THE WILD

NORTH

ION IDRIESS

With 24 Maps

ETT IMPRINT

Exile Bay

This 4th edition published by ETT Imprint, Exile Bay 2023

First published by Angus & Robertson Publishers 1960
Reprinted 1961, 1967

First electronic edition published by ETT Imprint in 2023

ETT IMPRINT
PO Box R1906
Royal Exchange NSW 1225 Australia

Copyright © Idriess Enterprises Pty Ltd, 2022

ISBN   978-1-923024-30-4   (pbk)
ISBN   978-1-923024-31-1   (ebk)

Cover: Photographs from the working archive of Ion Idriess

(courtesy Sydney Rare Book Auctions)

Designed by Tom Thompson

CONTENTS

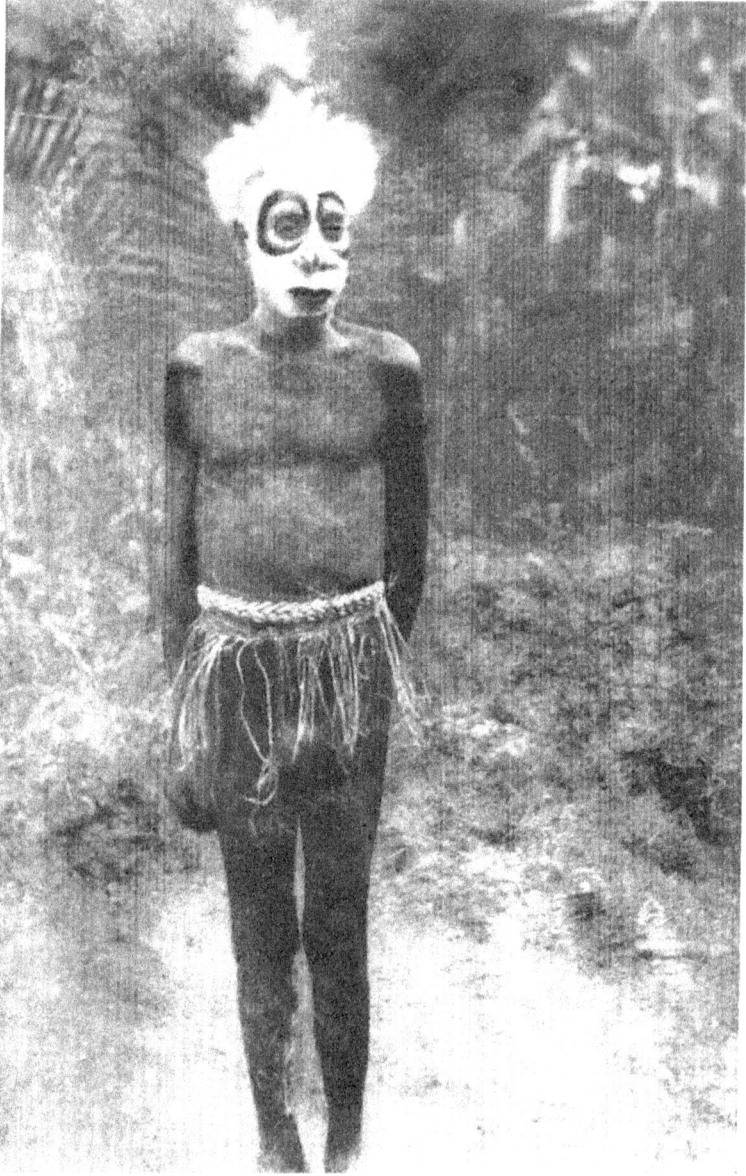

A weird-looking 'wolf'-boy to meet on a dark night.

Author's Note

I WAS going to throw these stories away, but changed my mind. After all, they were quite laboriously written "on the spot" during an intensely interesting period of Australia's development.

Few indeed fully realized how interesting it was; we were far too busy making our living in the growing little cities, or outback townships, or away out in the then wild bush. The telephone and motor-car and aeroplane and antibiotics and world wars and Spanish influenzas and submarines and penicillin and electronics and sputniks were all to come-coming with such bewildering swiftness as we toiled on, not realizing that a period in the world's history was fast vanishing from under our very hands. It vanished so suddenly-except in a very, very few isolated areas-that even the present generation scarcely realize such environment and conditions existed in this our own continent, in their own fathers' day. Thus, wondering over these old stories of youthful days, it also struck me that this thing then happening in Australia was happening at the same time throughout the entire world wherever there were "undeveloped" areas, as if some vast hand were slowly turning over the leaves of the Book of Fate, inexorably turning over the undeveloped leaf of North Australia, of "the Islands", turning over the leaf of Africa, of the Sudan, of Persia, of Arabia.

Even in such places as the Sahara the isolation of thousands of years, the frightful, waterless distances, the age-old nomads of the desert are all swiftly vanishing before the internal combustion engine financed by advancing civilization. What is left in all the world of the frontier life that was the bush of my boyhood days? The headwaters of the Amazon maybe, perhaps a "spot" or two in Abyssinia, perhaps some particularly remote or unwanted spot in each continent and out-of-the-way archipelago.

Thus, life as portrayed in these rough little incidents will never come again to our continent. I thought they could prove of interest to Australians born into the Space Age. So here they are roughshod as I scribbled them at the time. But as most of my friends the critics insist that I cannot write, I'm sure my readers will overlook immature craftsmanship. For the hand that then scribbled these lines by aid of slush lamp in a lonely bush camp, or by moonlight on deck of a smellful-lugger, wielded pick or axe, oar or tiller by day, never dreaming it would be called upon to earn its owner his bread and butter by book-writing.

So here they are.

ION IDRIESS

One of the "Sisters", the extreme summit of Mt Peter Botte.

1

AS WHEN THE WORLD WAS YOUNG

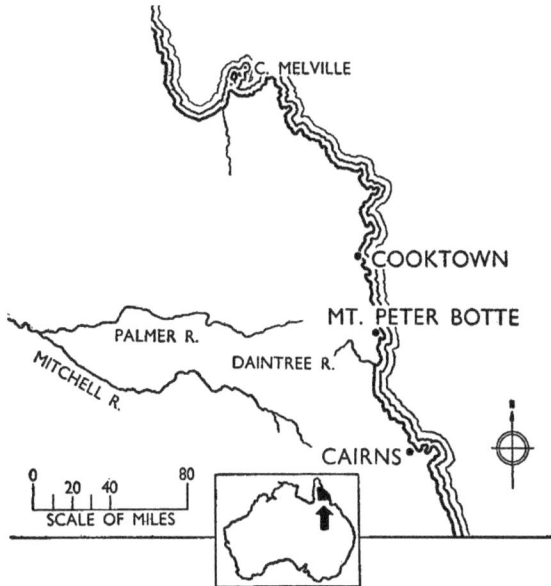

DOUBTLESS this story has been written a thousand times - how many thousands and thousands of times - in the actual lives of untold couples since man first came upon the earth.

The lucky couples - alas, only the lucky couples - suc-ceeded in vanishing with their lives still their own. Long afterwards their "story" would appear - a tiny handful of people, the makings of a new tribe, springing up every here and there far over the face of the earth. And amalgamations of such tribes that survived the centuries would be the makings of a nation. That phase of the world's history has now vanished, with the vanishing of many other things.

More particularly with the vanishing of the Australian aboriginal. For this story of Koo-gara is quite true. My mates and I saw a part of it. He and the slim, frightened mother of their children to be stumbled on our prospecting camp on one of the heads of the Daintree River (past Port Douglas, just north of Cairns) when at their last gasp fleeing from the tribal vengeance party. We made them welcome to what rough fare we had, of course. What they craved above all, though, was shelter, just for "a little¬ fell a time" until they could regain enough strength to carry them on into the unknown. And that they would do so the exhausted young aboriginal was fiercely certain, such unshakable faith had he in the protection of his Totem Owl.

They got clean away.

The vengeance party was hot on their now plain tracks, but exhausted also. We stopped them, they chewed their beards a bit and rattled spears in a growling rage, but we offered them a smoke-luxury of luxuries to the aboriginal - and put the billy on. They threw down their spears and squatted with a grunt by the galley fire; afterwards we felt certain they welcomed our butting in on their tribal affairs. After a feed and a rest and a sour grunt of acknowledgment they turned back for the river from our camp. They'd had it! And they now had the excuse to save face, for they could return to their river island tribe growling that the white men with their guns had protected the runaways.

Mount Peter Botte overlooks the now thriving Daintree.

At the time these notes were written there were only two white settlers on the Daintree. Now there is a butter factory and motor-cars on the southern river side.

But on the northern, Mount Peter Botte, home of the eagle-owl, that bold, windblown range still holds back settlement, the Two Sisters still staring far out to sea as first seen by a venturesome mariner named Captain James Cook. So, to the story.

Through inky darkness Koo-gara fled for his life. Feeling abandoned and alone at the bottom of the world, he hurried along up that Daintree gorge whose black walls arose to admit the sky but as a star-spangled ribbon above. The river hummed in its broader places, snarled with a hissing of ghostly foam where bouldery landslides had squeezed it into narrow channels. The hunted man whim-pered occasionally when he bruised a foot against a rock or slipped on a slimy boulder under water. Fear of the vengeance party caused the whimper, that implacable band travelling swiftly behind, somewhere - unseen.

Though the river walls had grown narrower these last few hours and the water shallower, still the force against him grew stronger as the mountain cliffs closed in. He was travelling with fearful slowness, this man-animal in a desperate hurry but he dared not leave the sheltering water, knowing so well that sharp eyes would then find his tracks by day. At last, with eager splashes of relief he turned towards the northern cliffs, where the sound of a waterfall betrayed the tributary creek he sought.

At the mouth of the creek he paused and faced down river, listening, his trained ears shutting out the rolling moan of the windswept gorge, the rolling moan of the windswept gorge, the thousand songs of falling waters, of countless leaves whose whisperings sighed down from the sky. There was no sound of man.

Intensely relieved, the runaway groped into the dense foliage draping the creek-mouth, hardly displacing a leaf as he stumbled farther in towards the waterfall. Determinedly he began climbing its dripping rock-face, gripping with toes and knees, elbows, fingers, and teeth, a helpful ledge here, a crevice there, a knob of stone higher up, a rope-like root farther along. Often thus, under direst stress, have men learnt to do "impossible" things. He was making a waterfall wash away tracks.

At the top of the waterfall this creek is a hissing, narrow sheet of water strewn with boulders, just the voice of water tearing through darkness. In the distance ahead, a musical tinkling told of another, smaller fall. He moved on, crouching, one hand gripping his spears, the other outstretched so that no jagged branch should spike his eyes.

So he climbed, climbed, climbed, with the roar from the hidden river below growing gradually fainter. He must climb so, for it is by a series of waterfalls that the tributary creeks tumble from the mountains to feed the Daintree River.

By upward stages the creek gradually lost its precipitous banks, its bed flowed in long slopes of diminishing water, wash-stones took the place of boulders. Flat terraces then formed its banks, clothed in an indistinguishable mass of vegetation.

Koo-gara had thus reached the highlands. He swung himself up to an overhanging branch, climbed along it, and slid round the tree-trunk onto an opposite branch overspreading the ground. He dropped lightly down into the darkness, thirty feet distant from the bank.

Whatever tracks he made now he could not help. And, at the least, he was twenty miles away from the killing. In all that distance, his anxious brain assured him, he had walked in water, he had not touched dry ground once, or a dry stone, or a log, had not broken a twig or displaced a leaf.

Crouching by the lawyer-vines, anxiously he tried to think. Instinct in extreme need had guided him this far. He glowed warmly as laboured thought assured him, "Yes! I have done right!"

Then terror, not of the darkness, not of unseen pursuers, clutched Koo-gara. He heard a plaintive squeaking that he recognized was some baby tree-kangaroo separated by mischance from its mother-and the tree-kangaroo was the totem of Wee-na-mee!

He had run away with her, his blood cousin, he had violated one of the sternest laws of his tribe. And now she was dead, her spirit, by all the religious beliefs of his people, would have flown to her totem to inhabit the living earth-thing so as to watch over those she loved until they, too, departed for the spirit life.

Koo-gara implicitly believed that the spirit of Wee-na-mee, his beloved, lived now in that baby tree-kangaroo, and that it squeaked for him. He crouched to the earth, hardly breathing. A firefly, green with ghostly light, floated by.

A grunt like a coughing bull echoed hoarsely through the timber. Koo-gara gasped, for that sound was his own totem call! In the absolute stillness that followed, an agitated, plaintive squeaking told that the baby 'roo had heard, too, knew that it was hunted, was terrified of this winged hunter of the night. Clumsily it came lolloping along, unseen but noisy, seeking its mother, seeking sanctuary, seeking ....

Quite expectantly Koo-gara heard the furry little bundle push from the vines, felt it nestle against him, and he did not say it nay. To him, this frightened little animal really sheltered the soul of Wee-na-mee - and his love had rought her death. With the terrified fatalism of the aboriginal he waited for he knew what must come.

Again came that harsh grunt, then the silence was swallowed by the swish of powerful wings and two great eyes came, eyes yellow-irised, big and round, throwing a baleful glare brighter than molten gold. Out shot short, powerful legs with thick yellow toes armed with terrible curved talons that gripped the baby 'roo: it screamed and bounded against the nerveless aboriginal. The eagle-owl, its massed feathers bristling, brought its heavy shouldered wings crashing down with buffets that Battened the 'roo and set the lawyer fronds swaying. The great hooked beak half opened and a frightful screaming rang through the jungle as its wings thumped the life from the baby 'roo.

Koo-gara had heard that cry only a few hours before Wee-na-mee had screamed thus under the spears of the vengeance party.

The owl stared over its limp prey, its powerful wings partly extended like the humped shoulders of a dwarfed, nuggety man. Nearly three feet in length, with a five-foot spread of wing, the thickset bird loomed even larger in the darkness, its upright bearing crowned by a broad face set with wonderful expression, its huge, phosphorescent eyes glaring at the nerveless man, its whole aspect speaking of courage and ferocious strength.

With a shrug, it seemed, it bounded upward with its prey and was gone.

Koo-gara understood so well. For the eagle-owl was the totem of his fathers - his totem - the slaying totem.

At break of day he crept to the edge of the jungle, his body scratched from thorns, lean of Bank, haggard of eye. He clutched his spears with the taloned grip of the totem-owl.

He peered from the jungle into the dazzling sunlight of the open forest pockets bringing him the call of birds, hum of insects, all the living beauty of the day. The outcast gazed away over the lower line of the mountain summits, then, as if throwing off an intolerable burden with the passing of the night, he left the matted roots of the jungle floor and plunged into the knee-deep grass of the forest.

Chuckling with the almost hysterical reaction of a successful escape he hurried until presently he was climbing Mount Peter Botte. Towards its towering summit the vegetation grew scantily, showing acre-wide areas washed bare to the rock like bald patches on a grey giant's skull. Presently there towered above him the Peter Botte Sisters, a landmark to mariners far out to sea.

Climbing among stupendous boulders, jumping rock--toothed crevices, hurrying with the practised steps of the aboriginal he reached the massive grey base of the rocks. Dwarf shrubs encircled these. A bleak wind swept across the summit as it always does, howling up amongst the clefts of the Sisters. Lichens and coral ferns clung to the granites, high up within the crevices there peeped leathery orchids, a small butterfly hovered over a bunch of hardy, parchment-like flowers.

Koo-gara monkeyed his way up between a precipitous rift resembling a giant's causeway which connects the two masses of granite. One hundred feet above him in the leaning side of that smaller great boulder is a dark cleft that might have been hewn out by a Titan's axe. To this he climbed up along a crack, like a lizard climbing the leaning wall of a ruin. Grunting with relief, he gained the ledge and threw down his spears. Leaning flat out, he lay on the ledge. He could go no higher; he was at his farthest limit.

Dimly he felt he was at the top of the world. The wind roared against that rock of ages, fanning him to a tingling exhilaration. His view in magnificence cannot be excelled elsewhere in Australia.

Far out across the misty sea, like a smoky toy, ploughed a white man's steamer. How Koo-gara hated the white men! Across the great blue he could plainly see the white sand patches and reefs under slanting rays of sunlight beneath the mists. To the south, far below him, was the broad mouth of the Daintree River, bringing a pain of longing to his heart. Beyond the silver stream there stretched miles of timbered coastline, dotted with sand-dunes like snowy crests. His eyes again dwelt lovingly on the Daintree, cradle of his tribe. Enclosed by jungle-clad mountains, the mouth of the river broadens after the great gorge strews its waters to the sea.

He frowned towards the southern bank of the river where, miles away, there showed a broad scar amongst the timber. The cursed white man again, greedy, insatiable, ever pushing out, now threatening even his jungle tribe. For at long last the rich lands of the Daintree were being put under cultivation.

Behind him, to the north, rose titanic ramparts of scrub range. Farther inland, he knew, was an isolated, dead-end valley many miles wide, falling far down into the earth. In that valley was a tin-mining camp. How he hated those fools who tore down his native mountains in their mad lust for a stone! Farther west, running into the interior, his heart-sick eyes rested on a loved sight. Limitless mountain peaks stretching away into he knew not what untold distances, home of neither white man nor black. Like a grey-green sea were the peaks, misty under cloud-wreaths, with below them the tops of the scrubs in ever varying shades of green, vivid with light green of palm and tree-fern. Rivers and waterfalls in honeyed profusion tumbled down those countless gorges. A primitive land, crying aloud for primitive man. It was to there that he had tried to race away with Wee-na-mee. Alas! How swift and true had proved the spears of the vengeance party.

Koo-gara drew a long breath, then lingeringly turned round to gaze down again into the Daintree.

For a week the outcast spied on his unapproachable home, clambering when hungry down to the jungle levels for brush-turkeys' eggs and pigeon meat, all the time evolving a "something" in his consciousness, preparing to obey some deep, hereditary call. Very lonely he felt now without love, without friends, without country.

One lucky morning the Spirit of the Sun cleared the mists early and showed the hungry Koo-gara the smoke fires of his tribe arising in thin wisps three thousand feet below.

Later, a dot Boated down the river and towards its distant mouth disappeared into the mangroves on the northern edge. Very keenly Koo-gara watched. Very lonely he felt. That black chip was a canoe. Regularly every morning he knew, it carried a party of women to the river-mouth for the daily crab-fishing.

All that day the wild man pondered, a growing excitement at his heart, a warming of his blood. Leaning far over the cold rock side he glared from shaggy-browed, brightening eyes across those miles of space to the uninhabited ranges beyond.

Those illimitable distances beckoned, as the Unknown had called his ancestors in the Beginning.

Before sundown he had realized his destiny. Squatting up there near the stars he felt like a god of creation peering out across the darkening skies. He lifted up his arms and laughed-to stare mesmerized by two living orbs of fire.

A hundred feet above, from a narrow ledge, there stared down moveless as the very rock the grim visage of the eagle-owl. In that starlit silence, man and bird stared one at the other. Then with a weak little laugh the aboriginal stretched his arms to the owl. "Totem of my fathers," he called in a low, hoarse voice, "be the totem of my children in the moons to come! Guard me! Guard me well and I will breed thee a race far from the hand of the white!"

In exultation Koo-gara gazed out over the night. For his reading of the omen was that his totem spirit had been with him through all, had guided him here, had shown him the mountains of desire, had fathered the thought in his mind. His sin then had been visited on the woman, poor velvet-eyed Wee-na-mee. Vengeance had taken her, leaving him alive and free. As he mused thus, a star spun from space and hovered brightly over the invisible mountains. "Where its light shines brightest, there shall my children be born!" he whispered exultantly and in an ecstasy of superstitious reverence lifted his arms to the great rock Sister which housed his totem owl.

Before daylight the woman-hunter was hurrying down the mountain-side. And the light in his eye was fierce as that in the glare of that savage owl. In early morning he was hidden in the mangroves down by the lubras' favourite crabbing ground. Through the lattice-work of bushes he watched the daily canoe being paddled ashore, his breath coming hot and deep, his limbs beginning to tremble.

As the women with laughing jokes leapt ashore and scattered out towards the mud patch his gleaming eyes sought Larayieh as if she were the magnet of all the world. And so she was at that moment - of *his* world.

She was a *ka-na-ri*, a young woman at full puberty. She carried the yam-stick and crabbing bag: a circlet of plaited reeds drew tight her forehead, a possum-skin belt Haunted the smoothness of her waist. Wolfishly he noted the challenging poise of her head, the confident swing of the hips, the little round breasts so ripe for motherhood.

As she stepped by his hiding-place he sprang out and grasped her, his eyes animal bright, his breath quick and hot through bared teeth. Even then he would have spared her for the startled horror in her face, but she screamed, and he brought his woomera savagely across her temple.

He caught her in his arms and clattered his spears with a triumphant yell towards the startled lubras; then, throwing his woman over his shoulder, hurried towards the mountain edge.

Instantly shrill cooeeing broke out behind him as the lubras rushed to launch the canoe.

Koo-gara threw his woman into an ice-cold mountain stream. They must hasten. As she revived, he dragged her upright and with threatening arm pointed up the mountain, his fierce eyes and bared teeth voicing an imperious command. She leapt aside to run and shrieked to the sickening pain of a spear jab. She reeled while she clutched her thigh, then, sobbing brokenly, she limped towards the mountain.

Of necessity, they hurried in that great climb, yet when less than half-way up he signed a halt to their panting progress and both gazed back.

Away down upon the river were dotted the racing canoes of his tribesmen. He rattled his spears and laughed exultantly from the mountain-side. Larayieh watched him, then glanced down towards the distant pursuers, the beat of their paddles now tingling within her the feverish excitement of the chase. Her seeking black eyes now measured this defiant man, she appraised his sinewy strength, the will to do and fight. With a quickening at her breasts she turned as if reluctant to his snarling bidding and hurried on, ever up towards those towering granite Sisters.

When away up there, against the base of the two great Sisters towering into the sky, he pointed out to her the land of his desire.

She gazed long towards those misty lands so unknown and so lonely, she realized with a falling of the heart that through him they were claiming all her future life. She turned at last and stared into his eager eyes that were asking the question of her courage and her womanhood.

She placed possessive hands on his chest and her soft black eyes smiled up at him. He dropped his spears with a startled "Wah!" and clutched her, staring at her brightening face with the wildness gone from his eyes, almost a homage in their place.

Standing thus, they took their last lingering look far down behind them at the valley of their tribal home. With a long sigh Koo-gara looked up, then laughed a loud, glad laugh.

Pointing up, he showed his woman. "See," he called exultantly, "the eagle-owl, the totem of my fathers, the guardian of our children; he watches over us from his home in the rock. He is with us in the spirit for evermore."

He snatched up his spears and hurried off down the opposite side of the mountain, heading towards the great jungle ranges already dim in the afternoon light. With a panting at the heart, but a smile in her eyes, Larayieh limped quickly after him, now following her man.

2

WANG TU SHENG

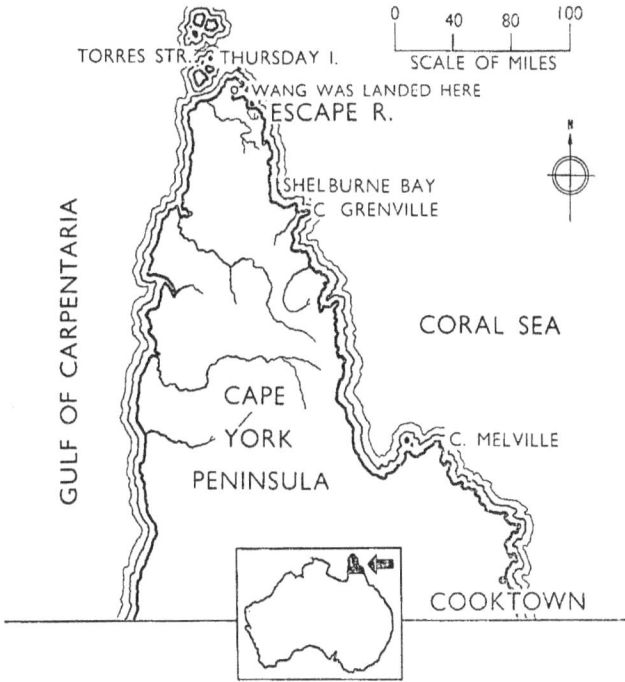

THE FATE of Wang Tu Sheng is a simple, quite ordinary little story in the development of our continent. Such incidents have been happening intermittently since the early Victorian and New South Wales gold-digging days a hundred years ago, right up to the present day - as witness the bodies of the two unfortunates found floating in Sydney Harbour in 1959; they had smothered in their own hide-out aboard the Taiyuan. Others also have paid a tragic penalty in this illegal entry of folk, particularly Chinese, into a new country of which they knew nothing but the rumour that it was some distant land of golden opportunity.

Hundreds, possibly more, must have perished even after safely landing during the hectic goldfields days in the North. For they expected roads leading to cities, a town on every hill, a village round every corner. Instead of which they were landed upon a continent of untamed forests and distances, with wild men everywhere. And these wild Australian aborigines did not like them. In fact, in certain areas it was the wild men's pleasure to chase, ambush, kill, and even eat them.

As to cities - well, there were only Sydney and Melbourne, two thousand miles and more from the coast where many of the Chinese immigrants landed, while the beginnings of towns were hundreds of miles apart. And nearly all were towards the south of the continent.

No wonder that many of these prohibited strangers, seeking a city in which they could quickly lose themselves, perished miserably in the bush. Very particularly so was this anywhere along the great northern coastline. Thus this story and others like it were quite familiar to us few who roamed the Far North seeking the elusive gold and minerals, sandalwood and buffalo hides, trochus and pearl-shell.

Wang Tu Sheng felt strangely alone as he watched the cutter disappearing into the northern mists. The risen sun showed him that he was encompassed by sea and bush.

Wang had been unlawfully landed there so that he might walk to Cooktown, down the east coast of Cape York Peninsula. Those vanishing Japanese pearl-fishers had quietly landed him here-for a price. He despised them, these brown-faced sailors of Australia's Coral Sea, and they had bidden him a laconic farewell.

When once at Cooktown, so thought Wang, it would be easy for him; a prohibited immigrant, to journey unchallenged to Sydney and lose himself there, in that city where fortunes are made. So with a last glance seaward he picked up his swag and started light-heartedly.

Poor educated fool! Cooktown, as the crow flies, was three hundred miles south - uninhabited miles. To walk along the coastline in the manner that a new-chum would be bound to meant a thousand. No wonder the little brown men had smiled sneeringly in farewell.

But Wang was a shrewd man, a product of Young China. In Shanghai he had trodden the streets arrogantly, clad in a tailor-made suit and patent-leather shoes, wearing horn-rimmed glasses, smoking gold-tipped cigarettes. He was the last thing in modernity, a product of "China's Awakening", he had been under fire, too, during the big student riots at Shanghai. He detested foreigners, for China, Young China, was the flower of the earth. Australia, so his class considered, was an uncouth land, but of magical opportunities-to the real man who could get into it. He was into it now, and the sands under his triumphant feet lisped a song until his aristocratic shoulders felt the weight of the swag. Little wonder, for he carried a month's food supply, and something else, too - £1500. Delightedly he smiled away the weight of the miserable food - £1500 in red £10 notes, while sewn within his shirt was a beautiful pearl!

A young man, he had already wrung from this foreign land the capital necessary to make him a merchant prince. Already he was that proudest of all things - "a self-made man."

So happy was he that he hardly noticed the easily negotiable beach disappearing under miles of stones where the sandhills gave way to a sheer headland. He smiled on, soon clambering over rocks, lulled by the sea on his left.

During these last twelve months Wang had been working at Thursday Island, Australia's northern pearling port, spirited there across from Hong Kong as an agent of the Opium Combine. Rich commission does the Combine pay to its successful agents. The pearl, though, was a private investment; a native diver, who was a thief, had offered it in Chinatown for £50. Wang had been the lucky buyer. But he grimaced at the thought of that £50. Fancy a heathen savage understanding the value of money!

He found the slippery rocks a little tiring. When the rising wind splashed spume upon his face he edged nearer the cliffs, momentarily annoyed. The morning wore on bright and warm. Seagulls screeched harshly as they flew along beside him on fishing bent, their eyes cruelly bright as they swooped low overhead. Sometimes he almost imagined those eyes were watching him; uneasily he shrugged away that old belief of the souls of men in birds. The rock pools looked the more inviting the thirstier he grew ¬what a pity those pools were salt! How clearly his face was mirrored in their crystal depths! A gurgling splash forced him to walk yet closer to the cliffs. He became very thirsty, he sweated, he rested. Strangely, he had never thought of a lack of water-water to drink. He had always got it out of taps before, or had it brought to him by servants.

As the swag grew heavier he rested the more, until startled by the tide hemming him in. He pushed on anxiously, seeing miles of slippery rocks behind and before him. Little crabs scuttled away, some stood antagonistically and champed claws at him. The water swirled, sucking in to his feet. He started to run. A broken wave knocked him off a slippery boulder and washed him dizzily among the rocks. He scrambled up, badly shaken, his arm cut on the oyster-shells. As he gazed at that warm crimson he sensed disaster.

He would have been fearfully worried had he known that he had travelled barely seven miles since yesterday ¬as the crow flies, only two.

With his back to the tufted coastal grass he lit a cigarette, and puffed his confidence back. He was not bad-looking, this slim young man with the sleek black hair, the black eyes almond-shaped, the almost delicate features, the olive skin browned by the Australian sun. But he looked out of place with the wild bush all round him, too delicately civilized to be out there alone.

He pushed on refreshed, regaining confidence as the wooded coast ahead developed into sandhills with beaches. Intersecting them, however, were scrubby hills that ran right down into the sea. Over these he had to push his way through stunted bushes and vines. The prickles tore his silken shirt; for the first time in his life he saw thorns in his almost white flesh. His swag grew exhaustingly heavy.

Evening found him dejectedly tired, alone with a terrible enemy; he had never counted on this devil that now trudged by his side, growing ever more real with the setting of the sun. When darkness shrouded hill and ravine and beach he staggered to a huge black rock and camped with his back to it - and then Loneliness spoke to him. He dared not light a fire; vividly he remembered his compatriots at Thursday Island warning him of the myalls. What if the wild black men really did come?

Glad he was that at least he had listened to his friends' advice and carried plenty of tobacco. The black men loved tobacco, he had been told; "nigger-twist" was good for "niggers", they would do anything for it. Tobacco might help him, it might even mean his life!

He welcomed the dawn as he had never welcomed it before; he had never really seen it before, anyway. He pushed on, gaining confidence with the light and the companionship of birds, the croon of the sea. He smiled as the heavy swag gradually cut into his shoulders, for its weight reminded him of the pearl. That he should be forced to enter this land carrying his swag like a coolie made him bitter. But the pearl would soon buy him a limousine. He halted, though, quite shocked at the broad mouth of the Escape River. He stared for an hour at that sheet of water ominous in its green depths, its history, too. He could not swim-what use, anyway? He saw a triangular fin cleave the water. He did the only thing - followed up the river seeking a crossing.

It was five days before he crossed the river and followed down the opposite side, listening for the song of the beach. He cried a little when he saw the sea again. He rested - he had to. And the cost of his exhaustion was a gain of five miles. Had he only known it, he had not travelled twelve miles, as the crow flies, since he started.

But no one could have convinced him of that; he knew he had travelled many, many miles.

He gripped his revolver, modern American it was, but now it did not seem to give him the same feeling of power nestling in his pocket, as it had when he was walking a city street. Each day brought its frights, only relieved, as he trudged doggedly on, by the sure, warm thought of his wealth. But the nights brought terror. He, this product of Awakened China, slipped back a thousand years in a month. The spirits of his ancestors watched from every bush, from every rock, from every sandhill. He had betrayed them, had thought them dead, those who can never die, who can invoke help even of the spirits of the planets. He had laughed at ancestor worship, at Lao-tze, at Confucius, even at the One Supreme Intelligence to whom this world is assigned. But that was in the cities. Out here in this great wild loneliness with the sounds and shadows of the night, it was another matter.

In a month he had not gone one hundred miles, as the crow flies. And yet from every hill, from every turn of the coast he peered eagerly for Cooktown. Bitter were his disappointments. His food was almost done, his clothes were rags, he was nearly done-no! By day as he trudged, by night as he hid, he was upheld by an ally greater far than any physical distress, any terror of the night-his fortune was a warm, living thing, £1500 in notes, those red £10 notes! By day his tired hands would feel the cool silk of those notes easing each dogged mile. By night he would pull out the notes, in the stillness he would gloat over them, smoothing them out, caressing them, weighing them, counting them, until his dreams, his waking hours, his thoughts, were saturated with £10 notes. And when the time of the full moon carne again, he called this pearl of his the "Tear of the Moon", for when he held it to the starlit sky it glistened so like the moon it really could have been dropped from heaven, from the eye of the Goddess of the Moon herself. For now, out here in the silences, alone with Nature and her whisperings, he grew to believe in the Goddess of the Moon, in the seven sacred things within the moon. Night by night he fondled that pearl, he nestled it in the cupped palm of his hand, smiling at its soft lustre. The pearl was a gem, it was worth £2500; but it grew to be such a companion to his loneliness, his hopes, that a value grew upon it even above its monetary worth: He laughed noiselessly as he held it to the moon, and the moon kissed it, this thing that was the disease of an oyster, this thing that had been thieved from a white man, that had been down the belly of a brown, and now a yellow owned it, he idolized it, he gave it a soul, his own!

And when despair seized him, with his food running low, so the value of the pearl grew and grew.

Thus he pushed on, up hills, over hills, across beaches, travelling from cape to rocky cape, from mangrove-tangled swamp to mangrove-tangled bay. Long since his neat light boots had worn out. He had bound their remnants round his cut feet with strips torn from his blanket. He had lost his sleekness, almost to gauntness. His body was a mass of cuts and bruises, his face was haggard, staring. He had lost, too, an invaluable thing, his confidence, his self-assurance. As he trudged anxiously along by day, so lonely that he seemed to have this vast world all to himself, he longed for that spirit of the days when in old Peking he had raved with a million others that China, that Young China, was the empress of the nations, the world her footstool upon which she would wipe the dust of her sandals in the quick years coming.

At such times in his thoughts he would halt, and gaze all around him. To his east was always the sea, its oneness broken at times by islands. But north of him, west, south, were hills, mountains, valleys, rivers, jungles, forests, rocks, sands-how frighteningly different from the teeming life of the cities! And always this mighty loneliness which he now felt certain was vindictively pursuing him. Away up by a range peak would come the far-flung, raucous cry of a giant black cockatoo. Wang would shiver and hurry on again, the beliefs of a million ancestors fast reclaiming him. That harsh, melancholy call, with a power that makes it ring far over the ranges - surely that could be no bird, unless indeed a bird of ill omen. And now, when he glanced at a rockpool spectres leered up at him from the bottom, even as they did from the magic mirrors in the sorcerers' dens in the homeland.

In these latter days as he trudged along, especially in these lonely nights, he was quite aware that the spirits of his ancestors pursued him. He had betrayed them, the first of his line for a thousand years who had failed to pay veneration to the spirits of his forefathers, to help them by prayer and offerings to the Celestial Intelligences that in return they might await him in Heaven and bear him off, when his time came, to his place in the Invisible Rest. Why, he had not even erected a tablet to his own father, had not burnt even one stick of incense! He shivered. He had turned Christian instead, it was so much less expensive, it was Westernized, up-to-date, it was Young China - he did not have to be really a Christian, it was simply a disdainful cloak that proved he had risen above the dust of those gone before.

And now here he was in a vast, strange land, a terrifying land, all alone. No, not alone, for in the breezes by day, in the call of a bird, the rustle of a snake in the grass, the gurgle of the sea in a rock-hole, he heard the voices of his spirit people, calling him, hissing. But at night they spoke to him, he would hear them cry his name; whisperingly, yet distinct from the dark would come the basest of accusations, all against him. As he crouched there in the shelter of a rock, in the Banges of a tree, in a hole scooped in the sand, their voices would come out of the dark. To while away the hours until blessed sleep came he would take out his wealth - and the Tear of the Moon.

Thus would come forgetfulness, joyous hope. For hours he would fondle those notes, no longer crisp, but smooth and sleek from his fingers, lingering velvet to the touch. At long last, with little white quartz stones, he would stack the £10 notes into the shape of a temple. At the very top he would reverently place the Tear of the Moon. Though the moon had long since gone there was always a star to seek the pearl out and it would shine upon the dull red note like a tear of the moon indeed. And Wang would kneel and bow with his forehead touching the ground before that pagoda of notes, and with the trembling fervour of a fanatic do homage to his ancestors, promising that should they but forgive and guide him to the land of men again he would devote all his life and his wealth to the building up of more wealth so that before he was an old man he would build in the Flowery Land a temple unequalled in piety and splendour.

So Wang trudged on and on, ever on, and his haggard eyes gazed, expecting Cook town to appear upon every hill, upon every beach, upon every river-mouth, upon every cape. He had not the faintest idea of distance, he was sure he should have reached Cooktown long ago.

He crossed Captain Billy Creek, he crossed a hundred unnamed creeks, a thousand hills, he followed the windings of Shelburne Bay, he could have saved himself a hundred miles had he known how to cut across country, but he followed the turn of the coast right to White Point, then followed its twist back to Round Point, then its detour to Thorpe Point, then right down into the mangroves of Margaret Bay. He struggled there with despair. Then the Macmillan River barred his way. He struggled along it many miles inland, plodded down its opposite bank and far away out to Cape Grenville. Here again, if the poor devil had only known it, by an easy ten miles' walk across country he would have saved himself a fifty miles' struggle.

When the last of his food was done he lived on shell-fish and oysters, and on roots and bulbs and berries from the scrubs. Collecting them delayed him still more. Sometimes he was lucky to find waterlily seeds and the petals of flowers. Eagerly he boiled them, tasting thus again the food of his fathers. How he wished for sunflower seeds and lotus seeds and chrysanthemums stewed with fish! The foods of his fathers seemed dear now, though the petals of the flowers accused him softly of the Moon Goddess - how he had once scorned her! Never once since his student days had he baked a moon-cake, filled with representations of the seven precious things of the moon.

He lived on berries and wild fruits, and poisoned himself. When he recovered sufficiently he crawled for a whole day through that tangle of undergrowth, emerging at sundown onto open forest hills.

His watery eyes rested on the sea. He gazed there, dribbling at the mouth, while softly the sun went down. He could feel his spirit going with it, he was nearly done.

With trembling hands he drew out his notes, slowly he built his penance temple. It was of value. It contained his soul and £1500 in notes and a pearl worth £2500. That temple which he built in two hours with his own hands was worth £4000 in good Australian money, £6000 with exchange, but it represented the wealth of the East to him, and in it he built his soul. Fool, the paper and the pearl would return to the muck from which they sprang, as would his body. But his soul, which he thought the least of, would live on for ever, and he was bartering it for paper, for money, and the material things, the vanishing things it would buy on earth.

He prayed until he mesmerized himself. He prayed his ancestors for a ship, a ship, a ship. And by midnight a certain peace had come upon him, for his ancestors were all around him. He could see their faces, staring, accusing, but not definitely condemning. Humbly he knelt to mother earth, praying forgiveness, praying for a ship.

In the first rays of dawn he was staring out to sea. He screamed long and piercingly as he saw the misty vessel. With a frenzied haste he set the grass on fire. The lugger would almost certainly be manned by Japanese and aborigines. How simple to bribe them to feed him, to put him ashore at night within a few miles of Cooktown! His signal smoke was seen afar by keen eyes, but, alas, on land as well as on sea.

It was nearly midday before the capricious breeze allowed the curious crew aboard the 'lugger to tack close in shore. As she put overboard a dinghy Wang staggered down to the beach. It was then that they got him. He did not hear a sound, though he smelt their animal-like bodies. He fell to his knees with an agonized cry as the spears tore into him. He knew nothing, did not hear the deep grunts, the scraping of feet, the animal cries. They tore his rags off as a starving panther might maul its prey. They cried in harsh delight at the sight of tobacco - it was tobacco they craved - they trod upon him, glaring seaward where the dinghy had stopped. It paddled rapidly back to the lugger, was hoisted aboard; the vessel stood off shore. The Japanese skipper, through his glasses, had seen it all. But he would say nothing. It meant months of wasted time with the Australian authorities should he report some lone wanderer clubbed by a band of myalls.

The heat of their passion gone, they pulled his rags to pieces, grunting their delight as they snatched tobacco. They knew what that was, butonly one understood paper. He had once visited a mission station. Eagerly he showed them. He tore the tobacco into shreds with his claw like hands, his shaggy face all laughter as he rolled the tobacco in a £10 note. He struck one of Wang's remaining matches and lit this cigarette, puffing triumphantly on his haunches. He puffed £10 away. With hoarse grunts of approbation they struggled for the papers. Many were torn in shreds. The Tear of the Moon was flung aside in disgust as they squatted there, smoking Wang's life away. A band of myalls from the wild west coast, their grease-stained bodies in nakedness, their hairiness not even covered by a pubic shell. Plaited grass adorned their biceps, nose-bones their nostrils.

Ever alert, presently they went their way. Their spoils were the rags and the tobacco and the little red papers of the murdered man. But before they went another savage noticed the pearl, the Tear of the Moon, and with him it went into the wild west coast. He would dangle it as an ornament from the nostrils of his gorilla-like nose.

The long, dry road into Birdsville.

3

LIZZIE

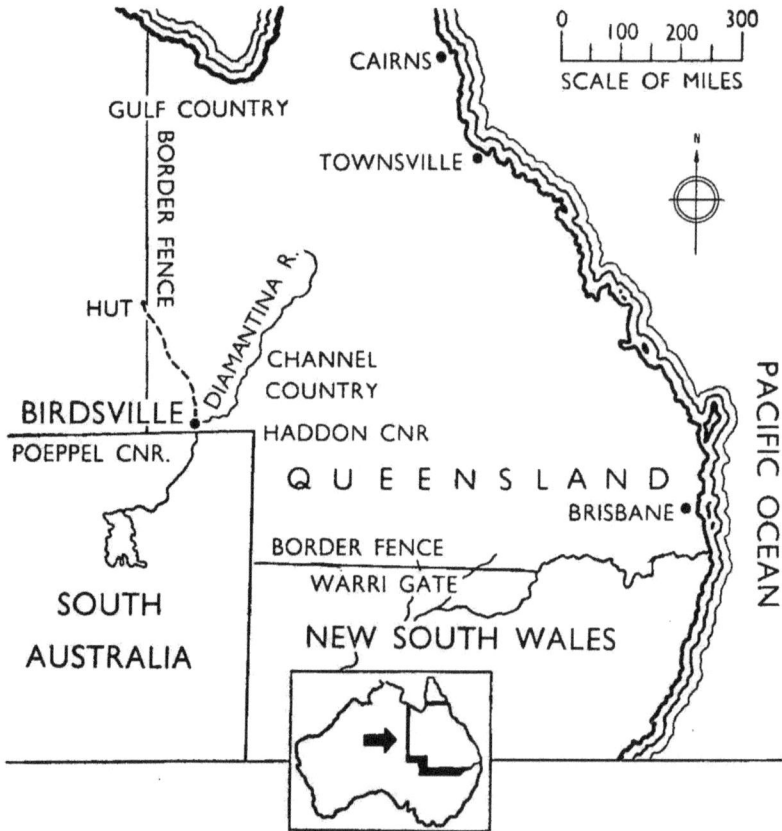

BEING a passing incident in the lonely life of the men who patrol the Border Fences. The period-those earth-shaking days when that Wonder Job the Ford was fast penetrating the back country. The "Lizzie" in question was the very first to patrol the Border Fence between Queens-land and the Northern Territory, to the dire prophecies of the lone riders, the snorting disgust of the horses, the contemptuous disdain of the camels.

Alack-a-day! Little did we realize that "Lizzie" and her tribe had come to stay.

Billy Gordon was proud of, was in love with, his Ford. In his sober periods, should any ill-mannered coot put his big splay foot upon the running board Billy would quietly dust that board down, his weather-beaten countenance wearing the expression of a pained Teddy Bear. A slow-moving, steady-eyed, quiet man as all are who become used to the lone silences of the far sou-west, he had developed through the ownership of that car an amazing boastfulness-though even so, only when he was not strictly sober. At such occasional times he credited that dust-battered car with almost superhuman qualities. And when he was really inebriated, well-there was nothing that car could not do.

Which was the way Billy felt on return from a holiday in Birdsville. (I remember Birdsville's one pub; a little bloke like me had to stoop to enter the door. By the way, in my time there the doorstep was a huge lump of browny-black ironstone, really the petrified skull of a Diprotodon. "As dead as a doornail!" one grizzled old drunk from the immemorial sandhills gravely assured me. "Been deader an' deaderer for thousan's an' thousan's o' years. Died fer want of a drink-an' now there's drinks orl eround 'im, an' the pore old bone-head don't know a thing erbout it!" Tenderly he stroked the shiny poll of that giant relic of ancient times.)

But as I was saying, when Billy returned back to his lonesome camp on the Border Fence he felt just that way - his Lizzie was the greatest car in all the world. And wasn't he proud of her! My oath he was!

Not so his mate Button gazing morosely from the hut door, though Billy was only a couple of days overdue.

Button, sheltering from the blazing sunshine of the sandhills, stood clad only in his patched shirt; he had put in time by rinsing out his trousers, the only pair he had since the dingoes chewed up the other pair. This pair of much patched bags was now drying on the Government Overland Fence, half a dozen crows perched there on each side of the necessitous garment.

"If them dirty squawkers -- on my clean trousis I'll shoot the stinkers!" thought Button morosely. "I wonder if Billy 'as killed 'imself in that bone-shakin' Lizzie. If 'e 'as the crows will be pickin' 'is eyes out be now-which won't do 'im no good. An' right when I want 'im, with Louey Foy moanin' 'ere with 'is crook leg."

For Button that day, with considerable difficulty and a cranky camel, had helped Louey Foy, the dingo-poisoner, from his mulga camp to the Fence Patrol hut. Louey had hurt his leg and swelling developments painfully suggested that the throbing limb needed the services of the A.I.M. Nursing Home at Birdsville. What good Samaritans those two isolated sisters had already been to the vast, harsh wilderness!

"If 'e don't come soon," thought Button glumly, "I may as well yank Louey up onter the camel an' lead 'im ter Birdsville before 'e konks out of blood-poisonin'."

And just then Billy appeared, honking through the timber, taking an ant-bed on three wheels.

"He's comin'!" called Button back over his shoulder to the sick Louey. "An' by cripes he's hitten her up, too! There's sticks an' leaves an' dust Hyin' from the wheels like hair from fightin' cats!"

"Can't come too soon for me, moaned Louey's voice from the bunk.

"Cripes! He's come!" yelled Button and, ducking inside dived under the bunk to a horrid clatter and shriek of brakes.

"Thought you was goin' right through the hut!" called Button reproachfully as he crawled from under the bunk.

"No jolly fear!" protested Bill confidently. "Lizzie can stop dead on a threepenny bit when I asks her."

"A bit tanked, ain't you?" inquired Button suspiciously. "Not me! Reminds me, though - Ie's have a drink." And from the car he produced several armfuls of rum-bottles, that good old square-face firewater of yesteryear.

"Lizzie prefers petrol," he chuckled, "but this is the stuff makes me spark!"

"You're not the only one," grunted Button a bit more hopefully. "How's things in Birdsville?" he inquired as they entered the hut.

"Not bad. Hullo?" Billy stopped in surprise, seeing Louey Foy.

"His leg's crook," Button explained, "swelled up fit to bust. I brought him in so as you could run him into hospital for repairs."

"Righto. I'll run him in tomorrer. How's it going, Louey?"

"Pretty bloody awful," groaned Louey. "Feels like a camel's hind leg with the dingoes chewin' into it."

"That's what old Post-hole Bill felt like before. they sawed his leg off." Billy nodded cheerfully. "You'll be all right soon as we land you in hospital. Gargle a spot of this, it'll do you good."

Billy got out the pannikins from the tucker-box while
Button produced a billycan of water.

"Here's luck!"

"Here's luck!"

"Here's luck!"

The first bottle hardly wet the tonsils, what with talk of exciting events in Birdsville. Old Abdul Khan, the camel-driver had stood splay-legged in the middle of the dusty road, torn his beard, raised thick brown arms to the skies and roared upon the Prophet to rain a plague of dead crows down upon Birdsville and all within it. And all because some joker had slipped a tin of pig's fat into his saddle-bag. Yes, what with talk of Diamantina Bill and Jimmy the Crow in the horrors developing the idea they were a pair of Siamese-twin emus galloping out into the Simpson Desert, what with gossip about the boys up along the Border Fence, time passed pleasantly by. When they had finished the third bottle they examined Louey's leg.

"Looks pretty crook," decided Billy gravely.

"Yes," sighed Button, "Looks crook all right!" Louey mumbled that he felt a bit that way himself.

By the time they finished the fourth bottle they decided that nothing short of amputation could save Louey's leg. Louey groaned in anticipation.

"It's all right," growled Button as in puzzled fashion he scratched his head, "they ain't started on you yet. Can't see how they'll do it, anyways. There's only two sisters at the Home, no sawbones. Sisters ain't got the tools, anyways."

"Tha's all right!" declared Billy comfortingly. "We can call at the station on the way in an' borrer the station butcher's tools. He's got saws an' knives an' axes for choppin' up the bullicks!"

"I never thought of that!" said Button in relieved tones.

"You'll be all right, Louey."

Louey groaned hollowly.

It was when they were midway through the fifth bottle they decided that only immediate amputation could save Louey's life.

"We've got to save him! Come on!" shouted Billy and staggered out to the car, hugging the last of the bottles.

"How about Louey?" called Button.
"Oh, I forgot him!" and Billy, turning back to the hut, tripped over his own shadow.

Button helped him up out of a cloud of bad language, observing airily, "Didn't know you had such a load on."

"I *ain't* got a load on!" roared Billy indignantly. "I tripped over that pack-saddle you left in the path."

"There ain't no pack-saddle there," said Button doubtfully.

"Well, I thought there was."

"Well, there ain't. I can see plain now. Come an' give me a hand with Louey."

Tenderly they seized the groaning Louey who promptly howled, "Ow! Owoo! Mind me bloody leg!"

"We ain't touched the damn' thing!" snorted Button. "Squealing like a stuck pig for nothin'! Just wait till old Sawbones yanks his tools onter it!"

"Up-end 'im!" ordered Billy. "We got to get 'im to 'ospital!"

They seized the groaning Louey now in reality incapable of walking, and manhandled him to the door where he banged his head, owing to some miscalculation or other when Billy fell over Button's feet. Quite angrily and somewhat noisily picking themselves and Louey up out of the dust they lugged him out to Lizzie and bundled him into the back of her. Then Billy leapt for the driver's seat and just made it.

"Jump in!" he yelled and started the engine with a roar.

"Hold hard!" yelled Button. "I want me trousis!" and he jumped back for the fence.

"Leave 'em!" called Billy scornfully. "What's trousers to a man's life?"

"A hell of a lot!" gasped Button as he snatched his pants and leapt back for the car. "If 'e ain't got 'em life ain't worth living."

A fat lot of difference they make to you anyway!" growled Billy contemptuously. "You don't look any different with 'em off or on!"

"I'm as good a man as-" snorted Button, but the Ford plunged off with a snort and a rattle, a startled, heart-rending groan from Louey.

"I'll soon dry 'em!" declared Button triumphantly. "The wind will fix 'em", and he held the trousers out the car.

"We've go to make speed!" shouted Billy as he shoved the old Ford all out. "We've got eighty miles to go and a dyin' man in the car!"

"My Gawd!" howled Button. "Hold her! Me trousis is gom! Hold her!"

"Gone where?" demanded Billy.

"Don't know-they hit that larst tree you hit an' pulled 'em orf of me hand! Stop her!"

"Can't stop her!" shouted Billy. "This is a case of life and death!"

"But how can a man face those women without trousis?" wailed Button.

"Don't face 'em-turn your back."

"Oh hell!" moaned Button. "I won't know which way to tum!"

Louey groaned in sympathy.

Across the needlewood flats the old car sped as if she just loved it.

"See how she barks the trees!" cried Billy delightedly.

"Now see me polish that ant-bed!"

He did-with a bump that nearly killed Louey and sent Button half through the tattered windscreen. But to Loney's anguished wails Lizzie flew on like a live thing to churn up and over and down the sandhills, to fly across the claypans, to clatter down the gullies and send the gravel flying across the stony creeks. Ever on again, missing hardy trees by breathless inches, the unfortunate Louey stretched out with a death grip on the bottom of. the rocking car while Billy, bent over the wheel, hung onto it as if for life, mouth shut tight, eyes glaring straight ahead.

"Speed!" murmured Billy. "Speed, we want speed!"

"We're gettin' it," murmured Button, else I'm in Dreamland. My Gawd, you're tanked! *Real* tanked. You'll kill the bloody lot of us!"

"Stop 'er! Stop 'er! Stop 'er for the love of Mike!" howled Louey from behind.

"She's a *car*," declared Billy passionately, "built for speed!

She's a speedy beaut! You've got to hang on by the skin of your teeth to ride her. Ain't Louey groanin' horrible? He must be bad."

"He'll be *dead* if we don't get there soon," hissed Button, "an' so will all of us."

"We'll get there," promised Billy as with gritted teeth he leant over the wheel.

Lizzie roared over a stony flat, bounced over a log, and skidded in the sand.

"Stop 'er, stop 'er! For Gawd's sake stop 'er!" wailed that anguished voice from the back.

"What's the matter, Louey?" shouted Button over his shoulder.

"Me leg, I'm dyin!"

"I told you!" yelled Billy despairingly. "He's dyin'! We've got a dyin' man aboard. It's a race for life." And he pressed the Ford on to its last long, wheezing gasp - which soon came with a shuddering, panting groan even worse than Louey's.

When from sheer exhaustion they gave up churning her Louey volunteered hopefully, "Perhaps she wants some petrol!"

"Of course she does!" laughed Billy as he dashed the sweat from his brow. "Who'd 'a' thought it! Everything must drink."

"I wish you didn't!" moaned Louey.

Billy got out the spare petrol-tin, emptied it cheerily into the tank, jumped in, and then, with a "Now we shan't be long!" Lizzie snorted ardently and hit straight out into the distances again.

"I told you! Ain't she a beaut?"

It was some miles farther on that Billy shouted,

"Button?"

"What ya shout in' for?" called back Louey. "Jack Button? Isn't he in with you?" "With me? No! Ain't he in with you?" "Of course he isn't! Where is he?"

"I dunno"

"Neither do I."

It thus struck Billy that Button must be missing. Unwillingly he pulled up and searched the car.

"He's fell out!" he declared in surprised tones. "Musta broke his neck. We'll go back and pick up the poor blighter an' bury him in Birdsville. Kill two birds with the one stone like. He can go in the hospital with you."

They drove back and found Button groaning in worried sleep under the scraggly shade of a coolabah-tree, energetic red meat-ants, big ones, just beginning to scamper up over his blotched, hairy legs, testing his meat with a snappy nip here and there in the tender places.

"Why, he isn't even gravel-rashed!" declared Billy in-dignantly, and kicked Button awake, now fairly busting with righteous anger. "You crawl under a tree an' go to sleep when a man's dyin' - an' I thought it was going to be a twin funeral!"

"An' it would have been in minutes!" howled Button, his yawn changing to a yell of anguish as he leapt erect with feverishly groping hands. "Here-quick! Pull 'em off! These damn' ants has tusks like elephants!"

"Pull 'em off yourself!" snapped Billy. "Why the hell did you have to fall out of the car?"

"I didn't fall off!" howled Button agonizedly. "Oh, these damn ants! You drove off an' left me when I went to put back the petrol-tin. Ugh! Hell an' flamin' Tommy!" He stamped agitatedly. "Give us a hand to pull off these flamin' ants!"

"Pull 'em off yourself!" snapped Bill, and bundled him into the car. They swung round and were off again to an angry snort; you could tell Lizzie was just about as angry now as Billy, having to go all that way back for nothing. Meanwhile the anguished Button was turning into a contortionist with howling accompaniment to bite of ant and bump of car, playing up shamefully, worse than poor groaning Louey.

Then an ant bit Billy - where it stings!

"Bang!"

When they picked themselves up Button remarked, "We hit a stump.

"I thought it was a mountain," moaned Louey. "What was it stopped the car?"

"A little fairy!" snarled Billy. "A little fairy with fangs like red-hot iron made me hit that stump! Why the blazes didn't you brush those ants off your pins?" he furiously demanded of Button.

"So I did," protested Button, "but there must 'a' been others hanging on!"

"An' you had to bring 'em in the car?"

"I had to bring me legs *with* me," protested Button indignantly, "an' *you* shoved me into the car."

"Legs! Call them knock-kneed shanks legs!" jeered Billy.

"Why don't you put your trousers on."

"I've *lorst* me trousis!" shouted Button. "The tree took 'em off me! I *told* you so!"

"Pity it didn't take off your head," declared Billy, "before you brought them ants into the car!"

"I thought you said it was a fairy!" wailed a bewildered voice from the back.

"So it was!" declared Billy. "A bitey little fairy playin' with Button's skinny legs made me hit that stump! But I'll miss it this time. Then we'll have a drink - I'm near perishin'." He backed out, then with a glint in his eye charged again.

Bang!

"If that was a fairy, moaned Louey, then I'm an elephant."

"You shut up!" roared Billy. "You oughter be dead!"

"I wisht I was!" moaned Louey.

Billy missed the stump next time and Lizzie staggered on. But to the experienced eye, had there been a sober one there, she was not the flighty miss she had been but several hours agone.

They negotiated another five miles at distinctly lessened speed but definitely increased bumps. Then Louey called, "Oh, Billy, the tyre is down."

"You be quiet!" snorted Billy. "A flat tyre don't make no difference to *this* car."

With a slathering rip the tyre tore and a myall root took it as the tree had taken Button's trousers. Sundry bumps to Louey's yells heralded the flattening of the rim, Lizzie stopped dead in her tracks.

"It's only a bit of sand," declared Billy confidently, "choked the gear a bit. Wait till she gets her breath, then you watch me make her travel!" He put her into low gear, started her. Lizzie roared, she thrashed the sand with a whirling wheel, there came a rip, tear, and bust as spokes flew in all directions.

"You've done it now!" said Button with hearty satisfaction. "We've busted the whole box of tricks."

"This car goes *without* wheels!" roared Billy. "If youse jump out I'll run over you. *Nothing* stops this car! She goes!"

But Lizzie wouldn't go.

"We'll have to walk," said Billy. "Hop out!"

"What - an' me with a gammy leg?" protested Louey. "It'll be gammy enough by the time you get to Birdsville," Billy replied with certainty. "It's thirty mile yet to go. An' the sooner we get there the sooner we'll get a drink -

because our last bottle is broke."

"No, it ain't!" declared Button triumphantly. "Because I been sittin' on one - when I been sittin' at *all*!"

"An' me with me tongue hangin' out a mile!" said Billy indignantly. "Perishin' for a drink, an' you sitting on a bottle like a broody old hen-with no pants on, too! You might have broke the damn' thing!"

"Glad I didn't," declared Button feelingly. "Anyways, I was up in the air most of the time hangin' onto this old bone-shaker!"

"You'll wish you was back in that old bone-shaker," snapped Billy, "when you're padding the hoof that thirty mile into Birdsville. Gimme the bottle an' hop out!"

They bundled Louey out, too, and soon convinced him that they were *not* going to carry him. With unbelieving moans at the base heartlessness of his mates he hobbled 'along with a hand on each man's shoulder. And some of his groans were real ones. With sundry drinks to oil the works they staggered along five miles, then shook Louey off.

"You're gettin' heavier every yard we walk," said Button indignantly. "You're poling on us an' groanin' in me ear. Your pins is as good as mine. Now use 'em."

But Louey wailed that he was being abandoned to die and sank down in a scraggly mulga shade, despairing head in his hands. His unfeeling mates staggered on until Billy turned and shouted, "Louey!"

Louey gazed up, Billy waved the bottle significantly, then he and Button turned their backs and plodded on. "Hey! Wait for me!" shouted Louey as he hobbled up and put a thoroughly scared energy into it as, with a horrid croak, a big fat crow flapped away from the mulga-tree and, planing low overhead, glared down at him from beady eyes.

"My Gawd!" gasped Louey to the brazen sky. "That bastard has been waitin' for me!"

The crow planed low overhead again and Louey shouted to his mates as he saw the sunlight glinting from that black, cruel beak sailing slowly overhead but a few feet above him. Instinctively Louey thrust upwards with waving hat, one hand over his eyes.

"Don't seem much wrong with his pins now!" remarked Button as he glanced back at the shout. "Ah!" He shrugged as he saw the crow.

"Ah!" said Billy. He waved the bottle encouragingly - which showed what a good heart had Billy. For it was the last drop in the last bottle.

By sundown Button's throbbing head was beginning to ramble back to the world of realities. The sting of sunburn on his bare legs helped a bit.

"I say, Billy, how about giving me your shirt?" he asked soberly.

"My shirt! What for?" demanded Billy.

"Because I've got no trousers. My legs is burning like hell."

"Well, I can't help that! If I give you my shirt I'll have none myself."

"But you've got your trousis."

"Of course I've got me trousers.

"Well, I want a shirt to cover me legs."

"Well, use your own."

"Damn it all, man. Then I'd have no *shirt!*"

"And what would I have?" demanded Billy.

"Your trousers!"

"Of course I'd have me trousers!" roared Billy. "And what's more I'm *keeping* them." He strode angrily on into the sundown.

Button sidled up to the suspicious Louey. "How about *your* shirt, Louey?" he wheedled.

"What about me shirt?"

"Do you mind giving it to me for me trousis?"

"But you ain't *got* no trousers!"

"Of course I haven't, that's what I want 'em for."

"How can you want 'em if you ain't got 'em?"

"Oh, hell! You know what I mean! I've got no trousers and I want your shirt to cover me bare legs."

"An' I want me shirt to cover me bare back!"

"Well, talk about mates! You're two fair cows of men! Why, I'll perish of cold tonight."

"You'll be warm enough when we walk up Birdsville Street tomorrow," replied Louey significantly.

And now it was Button who groaned.

The three wanderers spent a bitterly cold night huddled round a mulga fire, Button alternately roasting and freezing his sunburnt legs. Before daylight they were painfully sober, their teeth chattering in the steely dawn.

"Let's walk on," stuttered Billy as he strode away. "We'll freeze here. An early start will help keep us warm anyhow."

They followed him, peering for the track in the dark monotony of sand and claypan and saltbush.

"Every hair in me legs," said Button, between chattering teeth, "is froze stiff!"

"You won't be stiff when we come to Birdsville," snapped Billy. "You'll be so limp the dogs will bark at you."

Button groaned, picturing the dusty stock-route meandering up to the "pub-'n'-store" with the dozen or so little iron houses to each side. The inevitable horseman, half a dozen straggling abos, an inquisitive dog or two, the mob of goats, and the folk strolling out to have a look at "the boys comin' into town".

And Button groaned again, remembering this was the first time he'd come to town without trousers.

In mid-afternoon three very tired, dispirited, very thirsty men came to the Diamantina and saw the dozen lone roofs of Birdsville just ahead. Billy wheeled round on his mates shouting, "Oh, you fools, you stupid flamin' fools!"

They stood and gaped at him. The walk had been long and dry, the sun hot.

"You fools!" he hissed from clenched teeth. "You poor bloody fools!" He shook his fists at them, his eyes developing that maniacal glare.

"Take it steady, Billy," advised Button soothingly. "We'll soon be in Birdsville and shelter."

"Birdsville, you idiots! Shelter! Why, there's a spare wheel back there in the car!"

It took quite some time for the awful significance of this simple remark to sink in. When it did, Button sank down.

"This is the limit," he moaned, "the fair - bloody - limit!"

"Why didn't you remind me?" roared Billy.

"Remind you what?"

"About the spare wheel in the car."

"Well, that is the limit!" snapped Louey. "Your own car and you don't know there's a spare wheel in it! An' we walk thirty miles in blazing sun! And freeze all flamin' night!"

But Billy turned and strode away, swearing most awfully, towards Birdsville and sympathy.

Button snaked his way down the rough bank into the dry old Diamantina calling hopefully, "I'll wait under the bank until you bring me along a pair of trousers, Louey!"

But Louey trudged on after Billy without even one backward glance, one encouraging word. Trudged, past the little A.I.M. Nursing Home without a thought, let alone a moan for his poor, crook leg.

Louey, like Billy, had *had* it! So had Button.

4

AS A MAN SOWS

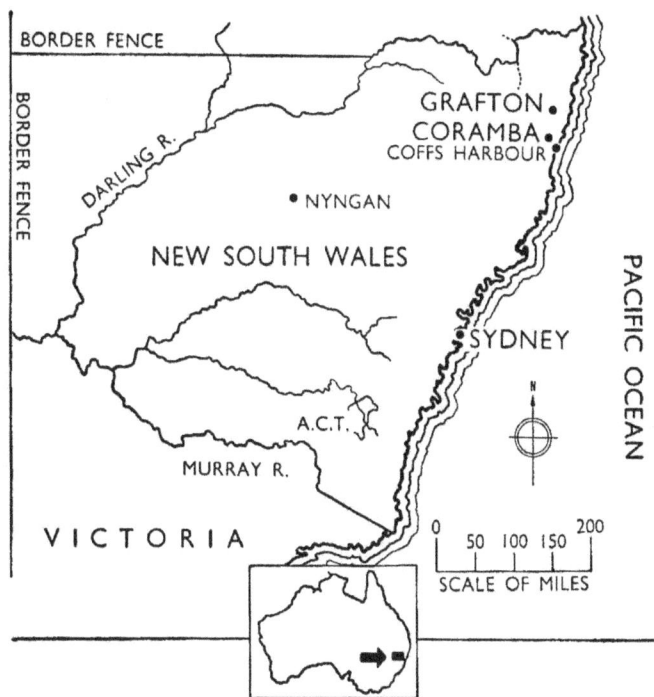

THIS simple little story, written "when my beard was black", tells of just one of those things that happen. Many of us describe similar incidents as "hard luck", or say, "Who'd ha' thought it!" Just simple little things that happen, that can break a heart at times.

Girls get queer ideas at times. I remember a pretty little bush township up Coramba way. The rollicking coastal range in the foreground, open hilly country all about cut through by deep, quiet creeks that never run dry. On the gentle hill-slopes the forest has been cleared to make room for the green fields and neat houses of the farmers. Each house has its garden, and in the season looks glorious with the rich gold of oranges. Contented bees hum among the verandas where the air is perfumed with honeysuckle.

At the back is always the white-painted cream shed, clean and cool. The cattle are always fat in that district, and Dad mostly owns a good-hearted though irascible temper plus a motor-car.

In one such house lives Irene Dallas, and she looks always as cool and sweet as the blessed prosperity all around. I remember at the bonny bush dances when I'd swing past her getting a queer idea of wild roses; whether the honeysuckle had caught in her hair or not I don't know.

Harry Logan might have, though. He danced most of all with her, and afterwards rode back with the bright-eyed girl through the quiet still bush to where her dad's farm nestled on the hill just round the big bend.

Harry was a teamster, one of us. His team helped drag the fallen forest giants from the big range down the long, winding road to the ever-hungry mill. Axes ring in those range fastnesses all day long. When the wind blows your way you can hear them ringing very sharp and clear if near at hand, echoing with a steely ring peculiarly their own when a good distance off, cracking dim and yet like a softly distinct bird's call when far away. Then comes a pause, as if the awed bush were momentarily hushed, waiting the fast-growing roar and crash that sets the very earth quivering and chases the disturbed birds up the gorges where the rolling echoes thunder fainter and fainter.

Then silence. And the crack of an axe again. And you know, with a queer feeling of pity, that yet another grand old tree has gone the way of all trees under the insatiable axe of man.

Harry Logan was a good sort of fellow. He whistled as he worked, and called cheerily to his well-kept team as they strained at the long chain that dragged the big logs up from the gullies to the bush track that led along the rough spurs and then down to the deeply rutted main road.

Harry dreamt of Irene mostly, even while he worked.

Whenever he saw an exceptionally good tree his mind in-stantly switched off in admiration of Irene, whenever his bullocks did well over a bad stretch of road under a heavy log he thought of some good trait of his goddess. Whenever in passing he admired a bright wild-flower he thought of something to correspond in his own girl and forgot all about the flower. It was a way he had.

And as the bush in the ranges among well-watered country is always very lovely, Harry had a bonzer life of it for just twelve months.

He was going to marry Irene Dallas, of course, and their selection was going to be the prettiest and best paying on all the creek, of course. Then one day -

I remember that day well because all the world was beautiful and I couldn't understand how any man could be unhappy until I passed Harry. Then I felt a dim sort of resentment because I wasn't in love, too.

The day was bright, with that cool sort of brightness when the sun's rays kiss your cheeks without heat, when you smile to hear a bird trilling far, far up in the air, as plainly sweet as if he were in the branch just overhead. When the crowns of the trees gently bow with regal grace as their leaves rustle to an unfelt breeze. When unseen insects hum without annoying all through the scented air and the horse under you trembles in his eagerness to bound forward and gallop until all is blue.

On that day Harry's wagon creaked down the long main road. Aboard was a mighty hickory log, a dinkum beauty. The bullock-team was pulling well and contentedly. Harry whistled a little faster, for they were rounding the Big Bend and the Dallas house would soon come into view. And Harry knew well of two calm grey eyes that would be watching the road from the house veranda.

The labouring team swung round the bend and began the descent of the creek crossing. With cheery voice Harry urged them up a little, for the opposite bank was steep and the up grade meant a long, heavy pull. The team responded willingly, as they always did, with the exception of Kruger. Now the strength of a chain is its weakest link, and Kruger was that link in Logan's splendid team. Not that the beast was weak in himself, he was as strong as any bullock.

But he was a rogue, and undependable. As the leaders splashed into the creek Kruger, half-way down the team line, sheered straight off and, exerting all his slow but great bovine strength and stupidity, attempted to pull the complete team off the track.

Harry yelled at him - he had just enough presence of mind not to swear - but the brute knew the master dared not leave the brakes as the clumsy wagon with huge, heavy log gathered slow impetus down the incline.

The leaders tried desperately to keep the rest of the team straight as they ploughed stolidly across the creek. But the rear bullocks were swung off their course and the big wagon, its brake screaming, slewed almost side on into the sandy creek, where it promptly stopped.

Then Harry lost his temper. He took great pride in his team, and for such a piece of downright bad workmanship to happen right under the eyes, and the critical eyes, of the only girl in the world - well, wouldn't any man feel the same?

Harry rapidly unscrewed the brake and, fiercely gripping his long whip, then and there among the swaying team gave Kruger the mother and father of a thrashing.

Calming down practically through exhaustion, he finally got the team, after three long, strong pulls, out of the creek and onto the hard road again. He was so furious and winded and glum that he travelled the remaining four miles to the mill without whistling once.

Next evening Harry, or rather the shade of Harry, came quietly to the teamsters' camp. We did not hear him whistle, we stared in surprise as he sat dejectedly down.

"What on earth's the matter?" asked Long Silver. "Have you seen a ghost?"

Harry only grunted.

"Out with it," said Silver. "In polite company this heavy silence is embarrassing. Have your leaders died? Or what?"

"No, said Harry miserably, "worse than that."

We glanced at one another in quick surprise.

"Then what the deuce is it?" demanded Silver.

"My girl's given me up."

We looked at each other across the fire in startled silence.

Then Silver's amused, hard brown face grinned.

"Get out!" he said. "The world's come to an end. Tell that tale to the marines."

"She has!" said Harry forlornly. "She's sacked me."

"What for?" asked Silver incredulously.

"Because I belted Kruger when he slewed the team into the creek."

We all roared laughing. But Harry looked up with quick fight in his eyes.

"What's the joke?" he said nastily. "Out with it!"

"A girl wouldn't sack a man simply because he belted a rogue bullock," said Silver soberly. "What's the real reason?"

Harry answered very distinctly, "She sacked me because she said that a man who would lose his temper and thrash a bullock would do the same to his wife."

It took us fully a fortnight to realize that the girl meant what she said. It's two years now since she said it, and she's still Irene Dallas.

5

THE ELUSIVE TURK

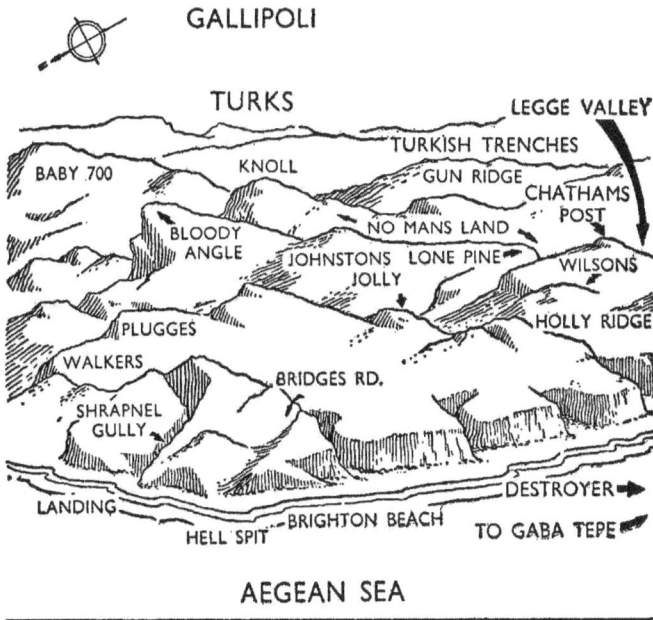

GALLIPOLI

TURKS

LEGGE VALLEY

TURKISH TRENCHES

BABY 700   KNOLL   GUN RIDGE

CHATHAMS POST

NO MANS LAND

BLOODY ANGLE   JOHNSTONS   LONE PINE   WILSONS

JOLLY

HOLLY RIDGE

PLUGGES

WALKERS   BRIDGES RD.

SHRAPNEL GULLY

DESTROYER →

LANDING   BRIGHTON BEACH   TO GABA TEPE

HELL SPIT

AEGEAN SEA

A SIMPLE little incident of the night on Gallipoli. Mostly, they were frightful nights. But my mate and I got a laugh out of this one-afterwards. Laughs were precious on Gallipoli.

We were out to catch a Turk. A thrilling job - we might easily land a Tartar! The "heads" wanted information - a live Turk with a wagging mouth preferred. Such was a source of enemy tittle-tattle in the early Gallipoli days.

So Alick and I "hopped the bags". Or, rather, we dived, so low and quick that our bellies scraped the sandbags and our chins the earth as we slithered down the sloping parapet and came to breathless rest amongst the clods and barbed wire and bomb fragments just out in no man's land.

No snipers' eyes had spotted our gliding shadows. The night was dark, but not inky black. The openness of the sky was heaven unfolded after the prison of the trench. The air was cool and sweet, except when tainted by the whiff from an unburied body. The darkness was cover, a cloak of invisibility, but, alas, not armour-plated. All was exceptionally quiet. Just an odd rifle flash here and there along the line, with, farther up towards Lone

Pine, the inevitable flame sheets and shattering explosions of the nightly bomb duel.

But facing Chatham's Post the night slept; Death dreamed. Straight down the steep hill to the beach ran our wall of sandbags, built by the men of the 5th Light Horse. The sea was peaceful and star-sheened.

Rising on stealthy toes, we faded into the night. I felt all eyes, and a prayerful desire that no misdirected bullet from our own men would thump into my back. The ground sloped irregularly, drear and bare except for an occasional foreign bush. About one hundred yards ahead a little gully meandered seawards, midway between the opposing trenches. This no man's gully was the rendezvous of raiding parties, scouts, spies, bomb-fiends, barbed-wire cutting parties, machine-gun "suicide" parties, and all the furtive desperadoes who sneaked out into no man's land by night.

We might ambush a Turkish patrol. We hoped to throw a sudden bomb, then overpower the nearest dazed straggler and rush him back to our trenches while his friends stampeded for theirs. That was practically our only chance of a capture. And on Gallipoli all was chance, whether the vast operations planned by the heads or the puny affair of a night patrol. Chance held the board and Death rattled the dice.

When nearing the gully bank we crawled forward, gingerly pushing the rifles ahead. The weapons were an infernal nuisance, as best friends sometimes are. At the bank we stretched our bodies flat out, our ears as well as our eyes expanding saucer-big, every sense strained, muscles ready for a speedy get-away back to our own trench. Homeless bullets whizzed carelessly by in any old direction, some singing that nasty, splitting crackle of the Turk, our own voicing a threatening hum that shouted of irresistible impact. Occasionally one would buzz right beside us, and its emphatic splitting on the rubble shrilled a definite threat. These flying bullets, aimed at no man in particular yet carrying death for any they might hit, were the very devil on a man's nerves. Barely a hundred yards ahead, indistinctly up near the black skyline, loomed the Balkan Gunpits. Those nasty Turkish fighting possies looked to be asleep, and we prayed they would remain so.

We craned our necks over the gully bank, listening. There came no soft pad of footstep, no whisper of alien voices, no snap of twig under careless rifle-butt, no smothered cough or sneeze or curse. We were first to the gully, this no man's gully. No one was waiting for us, so thankfully we settled down to wait - for others.

An eddy of air betrayed him. It shouted his presence, an incense-like whiff of Turkish cigarette smoke. It floated down from up the gully. He must have been stupidly sure of himself to risk a smoke in such a place. We snaked our way along the bank, nerves tingling, breathing held in check, every sense keyed taut, wild to win in that fascinating sport - a man-hunt.

We had crept but a few yards when the scented smoke faded away. We waited, praying that the fiend of desire would urge him to light up again. To venture farther might mean missing him, and, besides, every inch we crawled increased the risk that he would hear. There might be a dozen of him! Any second might bring vicious stabs from the dark.

Directly below us in the gully darkness, a shadow moved.

We did not see it; rather, we sensed a sitting form bending earthwards with cap shielding its face. The tiniest scrape of a match, quick hidden puffs of flame that reddened the ears of a man above a Turkish collar. Then darkness, and the shadow straightening with replaced cap and a smouldering cigarette. As he drew it alight the brightening glow shone momentarily on a sharply formed face with slightly hooked nose above a trimmed moustache. Then the cupped hand lowered the Judas weed. And the tell-tale air drifted the scented smoke up the gully banks.

He was alone, waiting under cover for those cold hours when sleep drowses the senses of men. A scout, probably, who would crawl to our parapet and listen for any whispered gossip that might betray the strength of the trench. Night-hawks preyed that way, on both sides.

He was our bird. We wanted him with a fierce desire.

Immediately we forgot Gallipoli, we forgot the armies around us, we were conscious of but one man. Before, we had felt like two rats out of their hole with all the world waiting to pounce. Now *we* would pounce.

We did - sprang straight down on him from the bank.

I grasped his flying arms while my mate snatched his throat and bent his knee into that writhing belly. He struggled like a frantic native cat, he bit and clawed and kicked and made funny noises with his mouth. His eyes were terrified. He was armed with automatic, gleaming trench knife, and a little bag of shiny brass bombs.

We felt secure when we snatched his weapons. We let him be, just glared down on him and panted for our wind. He wore the smart uniform of a Turkish staff sergeant-major. From the shock to already strained nerves, his dark eyes glowed like a cat's. He wheezed as Alick's knee eased from his stomach, then on the rebound spat up fair in Alick's face. The tension snapped.

Alick wiped his mouth with the back of his hand, and sharply slapped the sergeant-major's face. "You dirty pig!" he whispered furiously. "A man ought to run his bayonet through your ribs." The non-com's face sneered contemptuously, with his wind he was also recovering his nerve. His quick eyes registered our number, only two. He was calculating the chances, his nervy assurance warned us of a crafty fighter. "Youse no kill me," he sneered, "a prisoner dead speaks no information."

"Shut your mouth," hissed Alick, "or I'll smack it again - with a rock this time! You'd bring a mob of Abduls running down here, would you? Well, they'd only find dead meat. Pig's meat. Now hold out your hand!"

Hastily I bound Alick's wrist to the Turk's with a strip of puttee. Not until next morning did I tumble to that "kink" the cunning devil screwed his wrist into, which made the tying of him similar to tying a bent tube alongside a stick. The tube had only to straighten for the lashing to slip loose.

"Quick now," whispered Alick, "and we'll cage this shrewd bird - so shrewd he's blown the gaff that he speaks English, too. That's great. Quick march!"

But the sergeant-major was in no hurry. Every seconds delay, of course, meant the chance of some prowling Abduls butting into us. So obviously did he dawdle that I prodded him. He jumped amazedly and nearly dragged Alick down. A string of exasperated Turkish oaths made Alick's curses sound quite tame. His teeth were ivory white as his bulging eyes glared into mine. Alick chuckled.

"Look out she doesn't spit in *your* face," he whispered delightedly. "She's a naughty girl, this is, and she doesn't like cold steel poked into her pants. Quick march!"

"Australian dogs!" snarled the Turk. "You ees not the stale beer of soldiers! Girls' pants holds many a better mans than youse!"

"We punctured *your* strides, anyway," chuckled Alick.

"Puncture 'em again, Jack!"

I did so, harder than I intended, and Abdul sprang heavenward. He came to earth with such a crash that all three shivered in breathless silence, knowing that far less noise might bring volleys from both sides - with us sandwiched between!

But the silence remained unearthly, except that distant Lone Pine rumbled and coughed and grunted, the reverberations trembled under our feet - those deep Pine trenches would be about gully level, and were rolling with bomb-fire now.

Cautiously, Alick climbed the gully bank. I crouched behind the Turk, rifle slung, his automatic in my left hand and drawn bayonet within an inch of him. We negotiated the bank, the Turk in hollow-backed fear lest he should slip backwards, then, crouching low, we hurried for our home trench. No breathless schoolboys were ever more delighted at a successful raid on a farmer's orchard, no youngster ever exulted more over his first hard-won kiss.

The Turk stumbled. "Faster go slow," he whispered hoarsely, "by Allah youse will have them fire from both sides."

"Jab the cow!" whispered Alick, exasperatedly.

The Turk doubled forward, then cursed fluently. I couldn't help sniggering, and he glared over his shoulder and snarled back in Turkish and Bulgar. He was a game chap, but I suppose he understood just how far we would go.

Without warning, the night flashed into bright day; quick as thought we flung ourselves down. A thumping broke the silence-uncanny how men's hearts will beat under a terrible strain! Little pebbles nestling by gleamed quite large. Long lines of parapets leapt into view on either side behind tangled streaks of wire. And loopholes, loopholes everywhere, with behind them thousands of inquiring eyes staring out into the brightened laneway. We lay in the centre - petrified.

That blasted destroyer! Some nights she would glide close in shore and unexpectedly flood the Turkish lines with light and blaze away with her quick-firers. And the ant-beds she disturbed would furiously open out against one another, trench against trench in lines of flame, eerily dancing under the searchlight.

Abruptly the light faded. The world blackened. And still not a sound. Heavens above, why was there not one sound? We jumped up and ran; the Turk did not dawdle. Abruptly again the darkness vanished to eerie light. We flung ourselves down. A tiny earth mound attracted both Alick and the Turk; their heads met with a resounding smack. A string of curses in two languages was the result. I lay panting, quite motionless, but the angry Turk lashed out and caught Alick on the shins. Alick lost all control and cow-kicked savagely. That settled it. A rifle crack told that the night had seen.

A bullet whined into the mound. Before we were properly upright machine-gun bullets hissed around us. We rushed off as both trench lines awoke to blazing life. The Turk sprang sideways with a jerk of his wrist, and was racing back like a phantom. The blasted destroyer barked off her quick-firers and splashed the night with blinding flame and shattering hail of steel. We jumped down into the welcome home trench with the feeling that the complete Turkish Army was blazing at our backs.

Our catch got home safely, too, though he had the destroyer's shells to race through, for next morning the Balkan Gun-pits were adorned by a strange flag. It was a disreputable garment, and a brazen placard read, "It takes Men to puncture these, not Australians."

"Pity you didn't shove your bayonet right *through* his pants and further!" Alick grinned ruefully. "He wouldn't have been able to hop back so smartly then."

6

AS YOU WERE

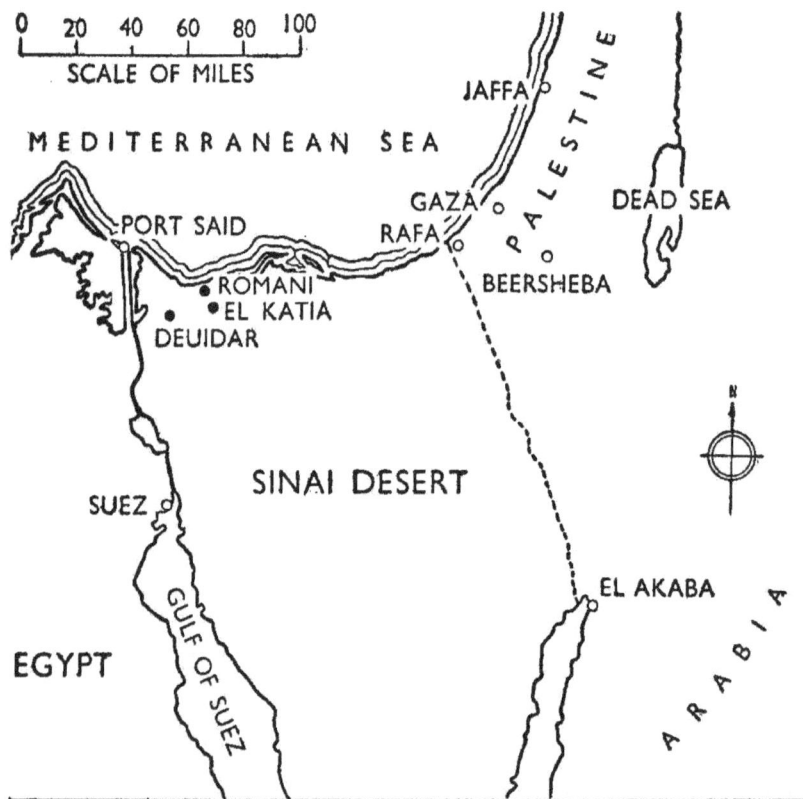

TELLING you a factual incident in the very uncertain life of an Aussie soldier during those hectic days before the battle of Romani.

The crisp desert air pulsed vim into Larry's bully-beef veins, skinny veins by now, like his long and skinny form. He forgot his dog-biscuit breakfast and fly-bogged plum jam, he whistled cheerily as his patient Aussie charger ploughed through the alien sand. A bullet smacked off his hat - both Aussies awoke and hurtled back down the sand-dune.

Larry rolled from the saddle with a "Struth!" his now alert hand on his rifle bolt. Great Jerusalem! To be actually sniped within our very own outpost lines-even within sight of the date-palms of Bir-el-Deuidar oasis and the regiment, of the camp of the whole brigade-that rough-living, rough-riding, 2nd Light Horse Brigade!

Leaving his trusty waler well under cover of the dune Larry mooched through the soft sand to recover his battered old felt hat, picked it up and whimsically batted an eyelid as he poked his finger through the neat hole in the brim.

"One half-inch further right," he thought woefully, "and I never would have seen dear old Aussie again. Nor Pa and Ma. Nor Bluey the cattle-dog. Nor the girl next door - bless her snuggly little curvies."

Making certain a bullet was in his rifle breech, safety catch at "action", ears and eyes now intensely alert, Larry began floundering back up the dune. Then, lying just below that brilliantly sunlit crest, most cautiously and gradually he poked up his hat until the crown just showed over the top.

Sliding back down the sand, blithely he muttered, "Now watch that, you eagle-eyed, misbegotten hawk of the desert! Watch that cady until I get the pleasure of drilling a hole through your thick chump of a head! *Then* you won't need your Bo-peeps any more!"

He stood up in hunch-backed alertness and, walking twenty yards along the dune, began carefully to climb again, on his knees, cautiously indeed as he neared the crest, then lay flat out, edging up inch by inch on elbows, belly, knees and toes. Grinning at his own cunning, he wrapped his haversack round the rifle in such a way that, at a distance, it would appear as a human head. Gently then, holding the weapon by the barrel, he pushed the camouflaged butt upward along the sand until it just peeped above the crest.

"*Crack!*"

Larry's arm twitched violently at the impact of the bullet through the rifle-butt. Urgently sliding back, he swore in emotional haste.

"Gee whizz! If that had been my head I would have been winging my way to the angels right now! You swivel-eyed bloody-well-wide-awake vermin-eaten son-of-a-gun!"

So his unwelcome visitor was a knowing bird - and a frighteningly dangerous one.

Disgusted by these unexpected events of this lovely morning, and with a growing uneasiness, Larry crawled back under cover down along the base of the sand ridge, then back up the crest to most cautiously retrieve his scorned hat. Then he slid back into temporary safety, all eyes and ears and danger-tautened nerves.

In the brooding desert silence that for ten thousand years has listened thus to the clash of arms in Sinai, not even a whisper of a sound - even though a brigade of men with their several thousand horses were camped among the sheltering sand-dunes only three miles behind him. It suddenly struck Larry that he might never see that brigade again. An almost overwhelming surge of loneliness struck him as" he thought of those laughing, sun-tanned faces, those two thousand beloved horses, the grim jokes, the tough, comradely life of the ever-moving regiments. And now, he might never hear, never see them again, might never again ride with his own section mates.

Unbelievable - but suddenly it was so.

Slowly turning his head from side to side, watching along the crest of the dune, he listened until within him he felt the phantom life in this desert air, as if it were filled with billions of invisible specks of singing sunlight. But no faintest whisper of trodden sand, no cautiously drawn breath of the killer creeping up the other side of the sand-dune. His wandering eyes, cold grey eyes now with a steely glint saw every leaf on a scraggy desert bush, every "pimple" upon the skyline of the sand crest before him. Yes, and he felt he could count the very grains of sand forming the golden, sun-splashed dune behind him. He and his patient old horse down their gazing so knowingly up at him, were certainly the only living things sheltering in this hollow between these little sandhills.

Where then, where was this *other* Thing? In the hollow over the opposite side of this dune? Or motionless, eyes squinting along his rifle barrel upon the crest of the dune yet farther away? Wherever he was, his deadly rifle had proved it commanded the crest of this dune, Larry's dune.

"To hell with this Abdul!" Larry frowned. "He's got me in a fix!"

Larry had a fearful respect for the real Turkish sniper - we all had - having long since learnt that seven times out of ten the crack of the Turkish sniper's rifle spelt death.

And he, Larry - "Lofty" to his mates - a fine scout *he* had proved himself to be! Riding away on a wandering patrol with a whistle on his lips and a pumpkin on his shoulders, and had not even ridden past our own outposts when a sniper told him about it with a bullet through his hat! Yes, a great scout! Sourly he thought of our far-flung ring of outposts that had allowed this scavenger of death crawl through between them. For Larry had to blame somebody. But all that mattered now was - where was *he*?

Larry gazed up into the brilliance of the cloudless sky that seemed to go on up and up for ever; he suddenly knew he dearly wished to see that sky again - tomorrow! He gazed away out over the golden dunes to where, miles away to the front a dark cloud showed upon the sands, the palms round the big oasis of El Katia where now bivouacked twenty thousand tough, grey-clad desert fighting men, with away on the sandy heights of Romani their outposts facing towards ours.

The enemy - and determined to come on.

But he did not fear those twenty thousand rifles. He feared one rifle - one only. And that one was very close, waiting - for *him*!

Thank goodness the old prad was safe! Affectionately he gazed down at the nag, and thought how he would love to be in that saddle again riding cheerily back to camp. He did not even dream of leaping into the saddle and making a bolt for it; such lunacy would have meant death for both him and the horse. What on earth was he to do?

There was but one of two things to do. Wait here in this sun-bathed hollow, growing nervier and nervier, developing all manner of fancies about what that unseen, stealthy brute might be doing, just wait here praying that lingering nightfall would find him still alive so that he could sneak away into the darkness. That, or else crawl right down into the hollow, then along the base of this dune, past its end and the end of the opposite dune, and try to come up behind his cunning enemy and take him by surprise.

On hands and knees Larry commenced that nervy journey, saw nothing but blazing sky and rolling miles of sand, heard nothing but the desert silence. He developed a thirst, an increasing anxiety, and a touching knowledge of the hotness of sand. Until - he had whipped up the rifle with sights lined before the butt was actually pressed back against his shoulder.

Just a mangy camel, a scabby brute, a weary-looking monstrosity with fly-sore eyes and a hunch like a silly sphinx.

This sorry sight delighted Larry, surprised though he was at not seeing the smart Arab steed of the scouting Turkish cavalryman he had expected and hoped to locate. Anyway, he must be right behind his man now, he had caught that smarty bending! And what a surprise he would give him! Oh yes, it was the Aussie's turn now.

With delight in his grim smile, Larry rose thankfully to his feet. How strange, what a puzzle is our mixed-up human nature! This campaign-hardened young fellow was a good bloke, willingly he would do any man a good turn if he could. At home among the locals he was good for a touch from the down-and-out any time, while the mums of the little township all had a smile for him, and every dog claimed him as its own. And yet now, in this beautiful day flooded with its silence of peace, there was death in Larry's smile.

Carefully once again he examined the rifle bolt. All was sweet. The camel squinted sourly. Larry, now facing the way he had come, looked up at the golden dune rising steeply above him-the enemy's dune-then dropped to his knees, and began to climb. His crooked left elbow held his rifle - the soldier's best friend according to the sergeant-major, he grimly thought - keeping the well-cleaned mechanism above the clogging sand as with elbows, knees, toes, and chest he wormed his way up to the slowly ex-panding sky. Near the ridge-top a handful of spent cartridge shells on the sand stirred him grimly. None of their leaden messengers had registered *his* number, anyway. He must be very near his man.

And now the razor-like tip of the crest stretched to right and left only a foot above his head. Drawing a deep, deep breath, and with rifle ready levelled, he peered over the crest.

The hooded figure rising above the opposite crest fired with the crack of Larry's rifle. Both figures instantly slid back down behind their sandbanks as two homeless bullets zipped past one another to whine away out over the desert sands.

"A bedouin!" thought Larry indignantly. "A dirty, lousy bedouin, not a Jacko at all! And, by heavens, he's got my horse! And I've got his stinking camel!"

Larry, as befitted a trooper of the 5th Light Horse, the "Fighting Fifth", had every right to be furious. To be sniped at, and to come within an ace of providing a bull's eye for a Turkish sniper was bad enough, but all in the game. But to be sniped at, and apparently outwitted, by a lousy bedouin, a scavenger of the desert, and his Sea-bitten camel!

"My horse!" groaned Larry.

Greatest tragedy to a light-horseman - to lose his precious, his beloved horse. But to lose it to a " -- bedouin"!

"He must have sneaked round the other side of the hill," thought Larry desperately, "Looking for *me*, while I was looking for him. Silly fools! He crawling round behind my hill, me round his - and we come up opposite one another! And he's got my horse! And I've got his camel! Oh Lor'!"

Larry had thought he had plenty to worry him; he might be killed any second, nothing in the world could matter until the job was settled one way or the other. But now he knew what real worry was, the probability of being killed slid away into the background - by hook or by crook he must capture his horse. If he were killed it would. not matter. But he must get back his horse. He dared not return to the regiment without his mount. What *would* the boys say? A lousy bedouin!

"Be careful! Be careful!" Larry's disturbed mind was trying to hammer back at his outraged vanity.

"Yes," thought Larry miserably, "he is a danger! Just as cunning as I am. And now I don't know who will kill the other first. Looks like our warfare has got us into a check-mate!"

Thus indignation was gobbled up by near despair, which in turn gradually gave way to cold common sense. He must do nothing foolish, for that would be the last thing he would ever do.

As the day slowly journeyed on into afternoon he switched his bad temper to a vulture that circled as a fly high up in the clear Sinai air. Full well he knew that vulture was lazy and fat and its horrible beak had dined plentifully on man and horse. It must know, too, must see for itself that many more such feasts would strew the sands when in a day or two those twenty thousand rifles across there under the palms in El Katia got cracking. "And me," thought Larry sarcastically, "me, one of the bright boy-scouts riding out to watch for any sign of the advance! It would serve me right if the whole twenty thousand of them came swarming over the sandhills right now and dragged me back to Constantinople to be a harem slave." Knowing full well what he must lose before qualifying for such a trusted position, Larry shivered the dreadful thought away. He'd die first!

Time dragged on and Larry began to feel still more miserably foolish. That cursed bedouin somewhere across there was not making one mistake either. If neither man became a corpse by nightfall, it meant he must trudge back to camp dragging along this mangy old camel. It would become the joke of the regiment, of the whole brigade, for months-while that atrocious bedouin would ride triumphantly back to the Turkish camp mounted upon a good Aussie horse! *His* horse!

In a flurry of vicious anger he just stopped himself in time; he had almost flung himself to the tip of the crest just on the chance of a shot. Heavens! And death so eagerly awaiting any such foolish move!

At sundown he spied a filthy white rag tied to a stick dejectedly waving above that opposite sand crest. Instinctively he knew that disgust and frustration were in every slow wave of that "flag", for his own feelings were keyed to just such a pitch.

His face was a question mark as hopefully he pinned his handkerchief to the bayonet point, then waved the flag of truce above his crest. Two brown claws, then shrouded arms, carefully rose above the other fellow's crest, slowly followed by a black-hooded head. Larry raised his own head; the reply was a tall body rising firmly erect in bold silhouette. Not feeling quite so brave, with mixed feelings, Larry also arose.

The figure shouted unintelligible words, waved a long arm that then pointed behind him, then expressively downward. Larry smiled delightedly at the thought of his horse. He shouted and waved back behind *him* down to that camel! The figure stooped and Larry ducked like greased lightning. But the enemy picked up his rifle, stepped boldly forward, planted the weapon upright in the very centre of the crest, stepped back and - waited!

"Well, I don't quite know for sure what's doing," soliloquized Larry, "but I must do likewise!" He planted his own rifle in the centre of *his* crest, stepped back - waited.

The bedouin nodded, hee-hawed his donkey neigh again, pointed away down behind him, then with the dignity of a sheikh honoured of Mecca strolled from view down behind his crest.

"Whew!" breathed Larry anxiously. "And what now?" But soon the bedouin appeared below, coming with long, unconcerned strides up the tiny valley between the two crests. He was leading the horse.

"Hallelujah!" shouted Larry in unrestrained delight.

"He wants his wretched old camel and I want my prad! Too *right* I want him!"

He fairly ran, in long, ploughing leaps back down the soft sand-dune to the camel. It was squatting now, glaring balefully. Larry "hoostha'd" it with a kick in the ribs and, snarling, it rose to its knobbly knees, pitched forwards and back, then stood in a weary lurch, with a harsh, roaring grunt belching greasy foam all over the infidel. Disdainfully then it shook its wrinkled hide and fairly showered him with sand.

"Beast!" coughed Larry. "You knock-kneed, scabby, filthy brute! How even a bedouin could come to like a beastly thing like you beats me! Hoostha! You slobbering brute! Come along before I belt the very daylights out of you!"

Between the two sandhills was now one dark sand shadow. The two men met fair in the centre. The bedouin salaamed as a Turkish soldier of the Crescent, Larry clicked his heels in salute as became an Australian soldier of the 5th Light Horse.

Solemnly they exchanged their snorting, mutually antagonistic steeds. Larry smiled in relieved, thrilled pleasure as his hand closed again upon those familiar reins. The bedouin, upright as a member of the Sultan's guard, regarded him a moment with the glowing eyes of a nomad. Once again they salaamed - saluted. Then turned their backs and each, with a shivery spine, walked away with his steed and dignity back to his rifle.

Neither man so much as turned his head. Mounting, both rode away into the fast-gathering shadows, Larry back east towards the brigade and safety, the bedouin riding west to El Katia and those twenty thousand rifles.

7

THE EYE OF ALLAH

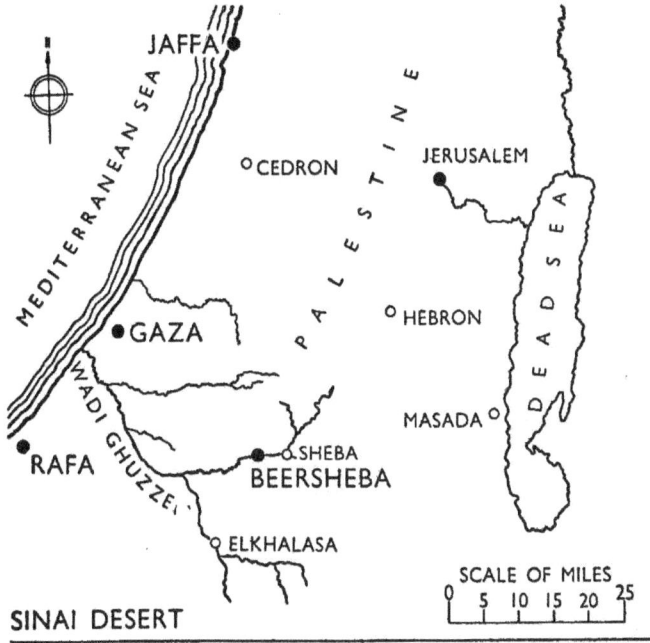

HIGHLY approved of by "the troops", our very own Brigadier-General L. C. Wilson, D.S.G., first learnt from a humble trooper's saddle in South Africa quite a lot about the cunningly efficient work of scouting - good scouting. Later, as an officer, he gained firing-line proof that the Australian bushman could beat the Boers at their own pet game. Which was saying something, indeed.

Years later at Gallipoli his scouting opinion of his beloved Aussies was confirmed. Later still came the Desert Campaign across the trackless miles of Sinai. The Aussies might well have been forgiven had those monotonous wastes of sand made barren their cunning and bushmanship. But with quickly won desert experience they conclusively proved that they could out-manoeuvre the nomad bedouin scouts, could throw dust in the eyes of the Arab "rats", and deceive the eagle eyes of the "Flying Camelmen" upon the very sands that had given them birth.

By the time that the barley clad plains and barren, rocky hills of Palestine had to be scouted and fought over, Brigadier-General Wilson (with many others) was emphatically convinced that his own particular men were the finest scouts of any army in the world.

Then he met his Waterloo.

One lone Turkish cavalryman upset the deep-laid plans of a Divisional Headquarters Staff whose brains had defeated a Turkish Army Corps.

Wilson ungrudgingly admitted afterwards that the grit of the lone Turk carried off the finest scouting incident that he had ever seen.

We, the ordinary Aussie troopers, felt much the same way about it, too - though with a sort of sheepish grin. Willingly we would have loaded that Jacko's haversack with V.Cs, adding a kick in the pants for having made such fools of us.

It was July 1917, when our highly expectant army was rapidly gaining strength for the decisive battle to break the Turkish line and push it right back to Constantinople. To which laudable ambition a heavily reinforced Turko-Austrian army had gloatingly replied: "Just come and try! Pigs of infidel dogs! Sons of Australian two-legged camels! Just come one step farther and we'll push you right back to the Canal and make eunuchs of you in the bazzars of Cairo!"

So that was *that*!

We had halted - Jacko the Turk *compelled* us to halt - on the desert edge bordering the first green fields of Palestine, that blessed green of barley fields after the burning sands of Sinai.

Our outposts were fronting the Wadi Ghuzze, which in Australia would be called a dry river-bed with precipitous banks twenty, thirty, and forty feet deep in places.

Some miles farther back from the Wadi, which was ahead of us, was the line of hills running from the grim fortress of Ali Muntar at Gaza on the coast, right away inland to the hills of Beersheba. Thus both armies faced one another, our outposts within reach of the Turkish and Austrian guns, replied to as occasion warranted by our own heavier artillery. The miles-long strip of level country between the two armies, stretching from Gaza away inland to Beersheba, was no man's land. And this was constantly being probed in hit-and-run fights by strong patrols of the opposing armies, the Turkish patrols trying to find any weak points in our line, we trying similarly to seek theirs, for the information of the army heads when the day of the Big Push should dawn. That was the position when, with both armies fast gathering strength our Divisional heads thought out a mighty plan to deal the main Turkish patrols a crippling blow. We should definitely blind their "Eye", then of course *our* Eye would be unopposed to see *all* things.

From the direction of Beersheba, daily our airmen were reporting large Turkish patrols hurrying out with the dawn, riding swiftly towards us and spreading out into the El Buggar-Kasif-Karm district, deep into *our* country, seeking what they might learn-and, incidentally, shooting at any of our own outposts they caught napping, and chasing the daylights out of our wandering patrols. It did not need the birdmen circling up in the skies above the scurrying Jacko patrols to tell us boys in the ranks this little item; we were sore about it, being forced almost daily to gallop home for our lives. And, believe me, a man *does* gallop if he believes that if captured he will wake up a eunuch. At that time, in that particular area, the Jacko patrols seemed to have five men to our one and they threw their weight about alarmingly. Which gave us a keen and immediate interest in this great plan of "the heads". We were all with them - for once.

The plan, and a really good one, was simply an adaptation of the stockyard wings trap for running in brumbies used in our own good old Aussie bush-on an enormously larger scale, of course. The "stockyard" would be a rough semi-circle of well-hidden troops. The spreading wings, instead of posts and brushwood, would be the physicallay-out of whichever part of the country was naturally suitable for the trap. Instead of the galloping, yelling, whip-cracking stockmen who would close the trap inlet immediately the frightened mob were galloping down between the wings, *this* trap would be closed by galloping squadrons of armed men. The only real difference was that our brumbies were not a mob of frightened wild horses but crafty, well-mounted Turkish patrols and their Eye - their scouts.

Thus we planned to catch these cavalry stickybeaks in a huge triangular trap, the "cheese" of which would be El Buggar. The "close in" signal would be a smoke bomb dropped from an aeroplane which would observe when the Turks crept in to El Buggar. On that signal our hidden squadrons would gallop in behind those confidently advancing Turks.

However, so well, so cautiously was this great plan planned that there was a proviso: if the trap chanced to bite off more than it could chew then the observing 'plane would drop three smoke bombs, which would mean, "Go for your flaming lives!" For the game was often "catch-as-catch-can" in Palestine, with the devil at the end of a Turkish lance for the hindmost.

So at eventide on 27th July 1917, the 5th Light Horse Regiment moved out, the colonel in command of a crowd of men all chuckling in anticipation of the huge joke we should play on Jacko in the cold, steely rays of the very next dawn.

Silence fell though, well before we rode past our own outpost lines, for the desert at night has ears, sharp ears. Any very few necessary orders were passed along by whisper. No slightest jingle of accoutrements from five hundred advancing horsemen. Miraculous? Ah, no, we had long since learnt how to ride without a sound. You learn quickly, when sound may at any moment bring you a hail of bullets from out the night. There was only one sound we could never quite silence, the murmurous sigh of hun¬dreds of hooves moving over the sand. And now this sighed away from, us as Band C Squadrons melted away into the evening towards their separate rendezvous, we of A Squadron towards distant Esani, shadows on the sand merging into a night growing quieter and darker with far overhead the blue Palestine sky filled with its wilder-ness of stars.

Only a hundred and twenty of us now, riding into the Turks' land, but carrying a nasty sting in our tail for all that. Fire-eating Major Bolingbroke was in charge of the squadron, four troops of expert riflemen, highly mobile, each troop with its own nasty Hotchkiss gun packed on a specially hefty horse. Tonight we felt we were invincible, for with us rode the "Suicide Club", the Regimental Machine-gun Troop, a tiny crowd packed with sudden death. In addition, most of us carried hand-grenades in our haversacks.

At this period of the Desert Campaign every squadron, let alone every regiment, had developed a brutally astonishing fire power. All the same, on this deathly still, chilly night our lone little squadron was not prepared to take on the whole Turkish Army.

Thus, far away out into the night over miles of enemy country the scattered squadrons were riding to form the Great Trap.

Our mob reached the Wadi bank at 9 p.m. Shadows crept up from a ravine and stole to the head of the column, shadows that were Sergeant Smith and his "boys", who had sneaked across there during the afternoon to spy out a crossing down the treacherous banks of the Wadi. Smith reported having seen well-armed bedouin soldiery nosing about on the east side of the Wadi towards Esani.

"Well, take six dismounted men and clean the birds up!" ordered Bolingbroke. "See that you do clean 'em up!" he hissed after the departing shadows.

The seven lads, itching for fight, quietly melted away and vanished over the Wadi bank. They snaked through the darkness across a stubbly field and presently caught subdued sounds of men working. They crawled on their bellies and, peering, saw shapes like giant bats in shadowy work among prehistoric animals. The boys heard a deep, rumbling grunt and glimpsed the outline of a huge, snaky head writhing back as a cowled bedouin crashed his rifle-butt upon its nose. The boys crept closer still, with itching hands upon their rifles, to those fifteen bedouin soldiery loading Turkish barley upon squatting camels. A bedouin hissed, "*Allah il Allah!*" whipped up his rifle, and fired.

The seven flew straight at them. Two cloak-shrouded figures went screaming down under the bayonet, another stopped a bullet in the brain and sank without a whimper. In a matter of moments the bedouins were "cleaned up". And the way now being all clear, A Squadron poured down into the Wadi and rode up along its inky black-ness, the hoof-thuds mufHed by the enclosing steep black banks. At 2.50 a.m. we spread out and halted in compact little troops absolutely hidden between abrupt hills two miles north-east of Rashid Bek.

Talking in infrequent whispers, we awaited the dawn, eager for what it would bring into the net. We knew that by now Captain Nimmo with B Squadron would be hidden two miles away right opposite us, and C Squadron would be waiting midway between, but two miles to the rear of, both squadrons. So the three squadrons formed the trap, and at its very heart was El Buggar, with the two-mile-wide inlet leading down to it, quite free of any sign of danger. In the morning dawn, immediately the Turkish patrols rode down the "throat" and were well into the trap, the watching 'plane would drop its bomb, and then the jaws, formed by A and B Squadrons, would close in to each other at a wild gallop while C Squadron raced its spreading flanks to close the circle. It was going to be a grand muster!

Dawn was slowly born in lightening streaks of grey.

Fog-wreaths clung tenaciously to the unfolding shapes of hills. Our shivering outposts, quite invisible from no man's land peered with eyes that saw in every bush a man. From high above grew the sharp drone of an unseen aeroplane.

Out of the dying fog ahead there loomed one solitary scout, his wiry grey pony stepping as cautiously as if imbued with the spirit of its master. Invisible behind him the Turkish patrols had halted in silence, awaiting what tidings that scout might bring.

On muffled hooves the pony came slowly forward as dawn rapidly brightened. Horse and rider halted as if one. The scout gazed at the open way before him, then at the hills flanking it on both sides. He could see no faintest sign of man, though hundreds waiting there knew of his coming.

Near him was a low hill with a flat summit. There on their bellies lay one hundred men of B Squadron, waiting, each with his loaded rifle stretched out on the earth before him. But only this squadron's observation posts could see, without being seen. They waited breathlessly for the scout to come riding down the "throat" of the trap and see what he could not see. No doubt he would advance as all good Turkish scouts did when approaching possibly dangerous country, slowly, suspiciously, very cautiously.

He did nothing of the sort. Allah breathed on that son of the desert and instantly he dug heels into his wiry grey steed and came hell-for-leather straight up B Squadron's hill! His pony flew up that innocent-looking hill like a mountain goat in the dawn. At the summit, with snorting gasps, it scratched gravel-for a second only because the rider instantly saw what lay there waiting and, swinging low over the pony's neck he flew down the hillside before the astonished squadron knew that he had been and gone. He got clean away. And our aeroplane, in futile spite, machine-gunned the Turkish patrols that, scattering in clouds of dust were galloping away from El Buggar back to the sheltering Turkish lines.

While we silly asses, tails' between our legs, rode sheepishly back to our own lines for breakfast, the usual bully-beef and dog biscuit - the prospect not being made more appetizing by the dust from the exploding shells now raking our flying squadrons from the Turkish guns.

And thus may one little man upon one little horse with his haversack packed full of active common sense defeat the deep-laid plans of an Army Corps.

8

THE BELLBIRD

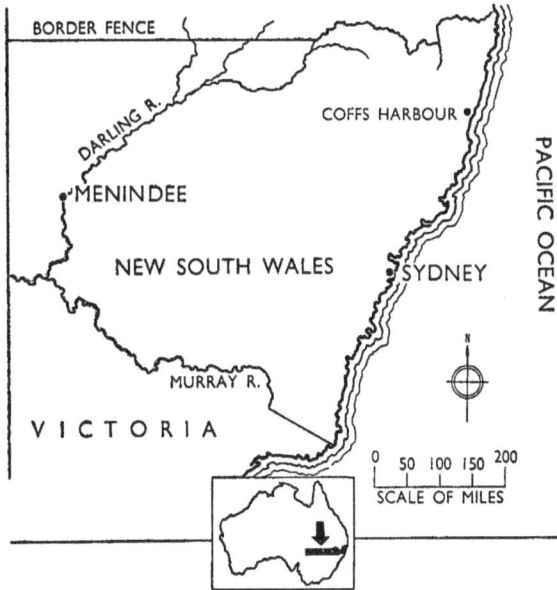

INCIDENTS such as this occurred - and still occur, alas - too often in undeveloped bushlands. Perhaps the bellbird may bring this tragically ordinary happening a little out of the ordinary. The proof of the bird's influence was plain to those who tracked the sick man. As to the rest, I have hunted 'roos in those heavy belah scrubs which in gloomy "patches" stretched along the border between New South Wales and Queensland before the excessive ringbarking days.

As to the fever, and the things that happen to a man's body and mind when he's "got the fever" - well, I know those symptoms only too well.

As to the vision of the girl, it was known that "somewhere back" in this solitary kangaroo-shooter's life there had been a girl. And that he brooded over the memory at times.

The sun streamed through the belahs upon the lonely tent. On his rough bunk of saplings and grass lay tossing and muttering a fever-stricken man.

He knew the malaria held him in a fiend's grip this time. He must struggle up and find a horse, then ride straight for hospital.

That meant an eighty-mile journey through trackless bush. He had best go right away, before the fever dulled his sense of bushmanship. He should really have gone yesterday, or the day before even, but the pride of his strong body and splendid health had made him unwilling to acknowledge that illness had downed him at last, that it was imperative he should seek the aid of others.

God! How weak he was! Head dizzy, legs shaky . . . and icy cold.

He staggered out to the galley and lit the fire, his hand trembling so that the water spilt from the billy. Dully he wondered if his hand would always tremble so. It would be a poor look-out for him if it did.

He gazed round at the old wagonette against whose wheel leant his rifle, uncleaned, and a bundle of kangaroo skins shot three days before. They had been good skins, too, spoilt now. They should have been pegged out straight away. Something serious must be the matter with him. He had never been guilty of leaving a rifle uncleaned before.

The tea tasted good, but he could eat nothing. Finding a bridle, he stood and listened, his practised ear waiting for the tinkle of the horse-bell.

But no sound came save the faint call of a distant bellbird. The horses must be away feeding in the open country.

He walked lumberingly from the camp, away through the silent belahs where the light was always dim. No wonder he could not hear the bells. There could not be a breath of air "outside". Even on the quietest of days these belahs were always whispering. His boots made no slightest sound upon the fallen leaves of this gloomy forest.

Presently he stepped out into the open bush sunlight, and the smell of grass was good. Soon he was walking over the rich green patch of grass where the horses usually fed.

They were not there. But a big old-man 'roo was, a red giant that sat back upon his tail and sniffed towards him. Thirty shillings in that skin! And he had no rifle, was too sick to use it even if he had.

He listened. Yes! No.

He swore, and turned angrily back into the belah scrub.

The horses must be away in there in the shade. He had heard a bellbird, and for a minute mistaken it for the horse-bell.

What a damned fool he was becoming!

It was deathly quiet among the belahs, but now a faint breeze made their wispy leaves sigh. Like the sighing of vanished people, his fevered brain whispered.

He walked for a long time, but could find no horses, could hear no bell, see no tracks.

It was becoming very hot. But then again he would grow suddenly cold and shiver with an irrepressible chatter of teeth. Curse the malaria!

He listened, ears strained. From far away came a low "tinkle-tinkle", soft and sweet and clear. He turned eagerly in the direction of the sound, right behind him. Yes, there it was again, a clear-toned bell, but a long, long way away.

He sat abruptly among the fallen belah leaves, hot face between his hands. What was this deathly feeling that had come over him?

God! What was that? He sprang up, wild-eyed. Breathing heavily, he stood fighting for control of his senses.

The noise was only a yellow-bellied goanna slithering up a dead tree. It sneered down at him from beady eyes, poking out a venomous tongue. His fool brain had imagined the lizard was Satan reaching out devilish claws that changed into a dead branch as he sprang back in affright.

The kangaroo-shooter trembled. How this fever racked a man's body! He wanted just to fall down and bury himself deep into this carpet of leaves, and sleep. He would have done so, too, but for some cold terror striving to keep his mind alive.

What a frightful plight should he lose control of his senses and wander forlornly in the immensity of this belah forest! He took a frightened step in the direction of camp.

But no! Camp was no sanctuary now, this developing fever would hold him helpless there. His only chance was a horse and a quick ride to hospital - if he could reach there!

He stood, gazing with a queer expression through the gloomy rows of trees. How cool and peaceful that hospital ward would be! He had luxuriated in one of the nice clean beds before. How kind the matron had been! And the doctor, such a decent sort. He -

The kangaroo-shooter shivered violently, pulled himself together - his mind would persist in wandering so. Fearful for his very reason, his listened intensely.

No! It was only that wretched bellbird again. He hurried on into the scrub, feverishly anxious. Where could the horses be?

Two hours passed. Cool here within this gloom, but the sun was scorching away overhead. Miles farther away, out in the open forest, the grasses would be drooping in parched distress. As his own body was now.

Thank God! Plainly came the soft tinkle of a horse-bell, quite close; he must have been walking and walking and walking and there were the old neddies handy all the time! Laughing gladly he half ran in the direction of the sound, peering eagerly among these sombre trees.

Strange! He could not see the horses. The bell had told him they must be very near.

Hark! There it was, the tinkling bell, a little distance to the right.

That was curious, the horses had never travelled in such a roundabout way before. Wild-eyed now, he hurried among the timber following that tinkling bell.

But there was nothing there - only silence.

A breeze sighed among the belahs. What a dismal moaning! These belah scrubs always had given him the shivers.

He shouted, listened, staring fixedly, beads of fever like unhealthy dew welling upon his forehead. Again he shouted, in a voice hoarse with entreaty, calling on the name of his favourite mare. Surely she would answer! She would prick up her velvet ears and hear. She always whinnied and came to him when he called her name - he treated her so kindly.

But no glad whinny answered, no thud of willing hooves. Ah, listen! The horse-bell! Tinkling clearly, musical in the distance.

Laughing delightedly, again he ran in the direction of the sound, repeatedly stopping to listen, knowing well the tell-tale tinkle would be repeated.

And it always was. Now away towards that low hill to his left, this time just to the right, sometimes straight ahead, then close by, again far, far away.

Despairingly he rested against a tree. "Hazel!" he called.

"Hazel! Hazel! Hazel!"

The sighing of the belahs gave answer, the bush seemed holding its breath. How often have I listened within that overwhelming silence!

"God!" whispered the man brokenly. "Where can my mare be?"

A brazen disc, the sun set. Like the bellbird it was right here, setting the whole bush on fire. But it was not, it was away across there! No, it was here ... it was far, far away.

"Tinkle! Tinkle! Tinkle!"

Exhausted, the man stumbled upon the bank of a gilgai waterhole. Gladly he remembered he was thirsty. Haggardly smiling, he tumbled on hands and knees in the mud and knelt to drink.

The gilgai hole was very low, almost a mud hole. The water must be bad, it held the blackness of decayed leaves and the stench of wild animals. And he had the fever! Of course, it would be bad for him, but a man must drink when he's thirsty and, besides, he might never taste water again. Not until he found those runaway horses.

Having gulped his fill, he stayed there, gazing into the muddy water. He felt much better now, satisfied and strangely happy. He did not wish to move.

Gradually, strangely, the water changed into clear crystal, fascinatingly cool and deep and peaceful. The bottom was a shade dark yet, but it slowly cleared, inviting the kangaroo-shooter to gaze into a mirror. A wonderful mirror, the rays of the dying sun intermingling with the silvered water in fading rays of red and orange and darkening shadow.

Gradually, with such a bright dawning of knowledge, the kangaroo-shooter realized that this mirror lived. For there formed round its centre a frame of happy memories picturing the face of a girl with quiet grey eyes sweet with sympathy.

How fragrant the orange-trees near which they stood, how brave the world on that splendid night!

Softly the kangaroo-shooter whispered, "Hazel!" Smiling, he bent to kiss his dream of years gone by.

He crouched back aghast as the cold ripples melted the face away.

But what was this? The mirror was reforming. He could not have been dreaming, after all. This time the frame was green and dull, like the walls of a long room.

Yes, it was a long room with rows of beds forming, white sheeted. Yes, and nurses, too, like shadows gliding from bed to bed, so quietly. He saw spots of red in the mirror, and smiled knowingly. It was night; those spots were lights in the ward.

On one bed lay a man - very still. The 'roo-shooter felt impelled to watch that man closely.

How pale the man was, though burnt brick-red by the sun! How limp that strong hand lying helplessly on the coverlet! A steady hand to aim a rifle, thought the kangaroo-shooter.

The doctor stood beside the bed now, dressed in cool white. He bent over the still man, then nodded at the nurse, who seemed to understand, for together they drew a screen around the bed.

The other patients could not see inside the screen, but the 'roo-shooter could! He was proud of his privilege and bent over interestedly to see what the doctor would do next.

But nurse and doctor glided away, leaving the still, sick man alone with the kangaroo-shooter: not quite alone, for in a wreath of mist a girl's face gazed protectingly down.

Suddenly, as the watcher looked, he was shocked. Uneasily he bent over, very close. There was something about this still, dead man - something -

With a frenzied cry the kangaroo-shooter sprang to his feet and plunged through the dark, dirty waterhole. Far through the scrub he sped, the night echoing in pathetic entreaty: "Hazel! Hazel! Ha-zel!"

Next day found the bush warm and quiet. A brown crested bird Bitted from tree to tree, calling in clear, bell-like tones, the perfect imitation of a distant horse-bell.

Inquisitively the bird crooked head sideways to peer down again at the maddened man who so persistently followed his sweet-toned call, a moaning, crawling thing that dogged the ever-receding tinkle on bloody hands and knees, clothes torn off, a bridle dragging round his middle.

At lengthening intervals the man would shout, but the bellbird did not know that the slavering gasp was, "Hazel!"

And the brown crested bird did not know why, though the man's mare did not come, he would listen so expectantly, his glazing eyes would gaze upward so certain of answer.

Much less did the bellbird understand that the memory of a loved one will draw that within a man ever upward, even though he be dying and alone. Even though that within the bellbird would have sacrificed life itself if necessary to save its young, still the bellbird did not understand.

9

THE OLD ROCKER

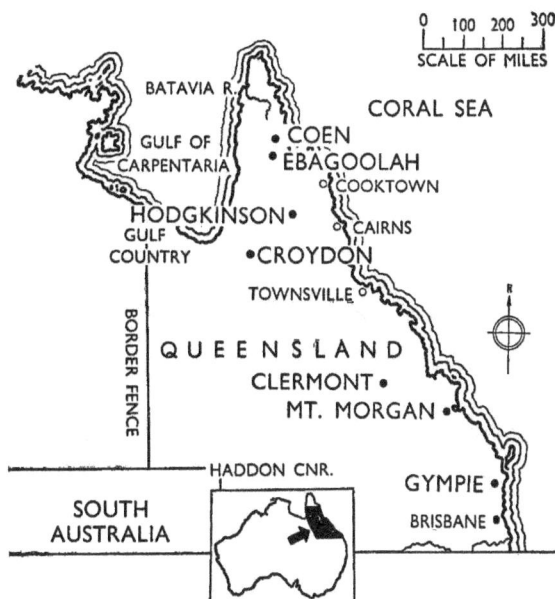

A TRUE little story, if I may call it a story.Life was a bit of a struggle for all our parents, when my schoolmates and I were boys and girls. The comfortable old rocking chair then in every home has gone out of fashion. As, much more fortunately, have those bitter days that at times came to the unfortunate among us.

Mum is a softie. Us kids know it. So does Dad, and tells Mum about it. Her softness gets Dad's back up. But Mum got even with him. She didn't mean to. Mum's too soft to hurt even Dad's feelings. The rocking chair did that. And made Mum laugh.

But Mum laughs so soft an' nice you just got to laugh with her, even if you've fallen off the chair. You'd be sure to fall off *that* chair. Everyone did. Everyone who sat on it sat on the floor.

Mum bought the chair. That is, Mrs Nextdoor bought it for her. She's sold Mum that way before. She just called over the fence: "Oh, Mrs Softie! There's a sale down at Mrs Diehard's. Her poor husban's gone batty, thinks he's a polytician. They're takin' him to the mad-house. Not the one in Macquarie Street! They're sellin' her up an' she needs all the help we can give.

I bought two chairs becos they cost me nearly nothing. But I only want one. A bonzer high-backed one for three shillin's, an' a rocker for five. I wisht you'd take the rocker. I was sure you would, otherwise they wouldn't sell the chairs separate. The poor woman is right down an' out an' hasn't got a stitch to her back, and 'tween you an' me she could do with some in front, too!"

Now Mum didn't want a rocker chair. Dad can make all the chairs Mum wants - when he's got time. Wonderful the things Dad makes with time! Shadow things.

But Mum's a softie. She bought the chair, an' a growlin' from Dad. Dad loves growlin' at people, 'cept policemen.

Dad was still growlin' when he sat on the chair. It sat him on the Boor-an' he roared. Dad always was a bear. Even his head's bare. An' you'd ha' thought he was that way where he sat down - as if Mum orter been handy with a cushin.

It was a home-made chair; its rockers looked like they'd lulled Noah to sleep when he was a kid like us. It was shaped like nothing at all and sat worse. That is, you never sat at all. Not on the chair. On the floor!

That chair wasn't built to be sat on. Which was how Dad treated Mum. An' snorted when the chair treated him similar! When you bent over that chair the seat sort of slid from under the back, banged your head, an' you saw the stars from the floor. Or on the little knob ole Nosey-Bob at school says our tails was grafted on one time.

It was like balancing Blondin, without the balance. If your mouth was talking while you flopped down to sit your mouth snapped shut as you hit the floor. All in one act. These newfangled fissychologists in the sixth-class boys would call it "telepathic intuition contacted by the lower extremities".

That's not what Dad called it, though! He'd just en¬joyed a big dinner an' was growlin' at Mum spending his hard-earned cash on paralysed furniture and flopped down into the chair with his mouth still growling.

It shut with a "*Whouff!*" Dad is heavy an' the floor thudded. So did Dad! The old horsehair patch as the chair creaked back an' forwards seemed to say, "Ha! Ha!" We laughed. Loud!

Dad didn't. The first "Haw! Haw!" wiped the daydream from his brow and he rose. So did we! Immediately, if not sooner. Down the back yard - leavin' Mum to fight the battle.

Mum always is left. She's a bonzer rearguard. She's a bonzer cook, too, and knows what to give a feller when he's got the stummick-ache.

Mum laughed. She couldn't help it. But Mum laughs nicely. You want to kiss Mum when she laughs like that. The lines all go out of her face an' she nearly has a dimple. She just sat there (not in the rocker) and giggled, all tears an' little laughs and coos of sympathy trickling down her face. I was glad the rocker had adopted us. Mum don't get too many laughs.

Dad dropped his hand off where he sat down an' rushed out into the yard for the axe. He'd make kindlin' of the damn' rocker! Mum encouraged him. Mum has tack. She humours Dad.

Dad roared then that he'd be damned if he'd destroy things he'd slaved to buy. She'd bought her chair an' she'd bally well sit on it!

Mum did! Next day. Quite unthinking. Until she sat on the floor. Not a big thud like Dad, but a gentle one, like! She sat there an' laughed an' the ole torn whiskers in the back of the chair creaked to an' fro in sympathy. There grew a liking between Mum an' that chair. It was human-like, how they took to one another. At least, not the chair. It never stuck to anybody.

It was great the way visitors fell for that chair. Then for the floor. Mother was goin' to hide the rocker in the kitchen. But us kids wouldn't let her. It was better'n a movie show. An' we never had to pay. The sitter did that. In dignity!

So Mum always warned visitors, "Please don't sit on the rocker. It won't sit."

But Mum forgot sometimes. She was so easily flustered. Especially when a "big" visitor called. That's how the parson came such a thud. An' the landlord! The parson said, "D-dear me!" The landlord said, "Damn hell an' blazes!" and picked hisself up an' slammed the front door.

Dad took to bein' grim about that chair. Growled he knew why Tom Diehard went mad. An' darkly hinted Tom wasn't the only man that rocker would send off his rocker.

Mum often laughed, quiet like, when she looked at the old rocker. Especially when Dad wasn't there. When us kids went off to school she'd sit in the old sittin'-room and she an' the rocker'd laugh together. I know! Because I came home early one afternoon an' peeped through the window an' caught them at it.

That was a bonzer ole chair. I useter sneak in sometimes when the others was havin' tea an' pat the ole worn arms. They was like Mother's arms, them rocker arms. They'd been plush once. An' pretty an' soft an' warm an' plump, like Mother's useter be, I'll bet. I useter dream that when I was a man I'd buy Mum a servy girl to do the washin', and fresh plush for the ole rocker chair an' just let them two sit an' chuckle together all day long.

The only day Dad laughed at the rocker was when the bailiff come. He went straight for the rocker. We held our breath. We'd been solemn like before. When the bailiff sat on the floor the rocker creaked back an' forwards like as if it was laughin' fit to bust. Only you couldn't hear it laugh for Dad's roars. We all laughed. Even Mum. But she cried a bit, too. She always was a softie.

But the bailiff was a sport. When sale day come, Mum carried the ole rocker down the back yard an' he didn't look.

Mum wanted to give the rocker to a friend. She couldn't bear a stranger havin' it. Dad blustered, "Why don't you pass it over to Mrs Nextdoor an' get it again when we settle down?"

Mum said that was dishonest. But nobody wanted the rocker, not even as a gift. I 'spose because it was like us. Broke. So Mum gave it to the bottle-oh. An' she cried. An' I felt solemn like, an' went an' sat down behind the old shed.

10

THE LUCKY OPAL

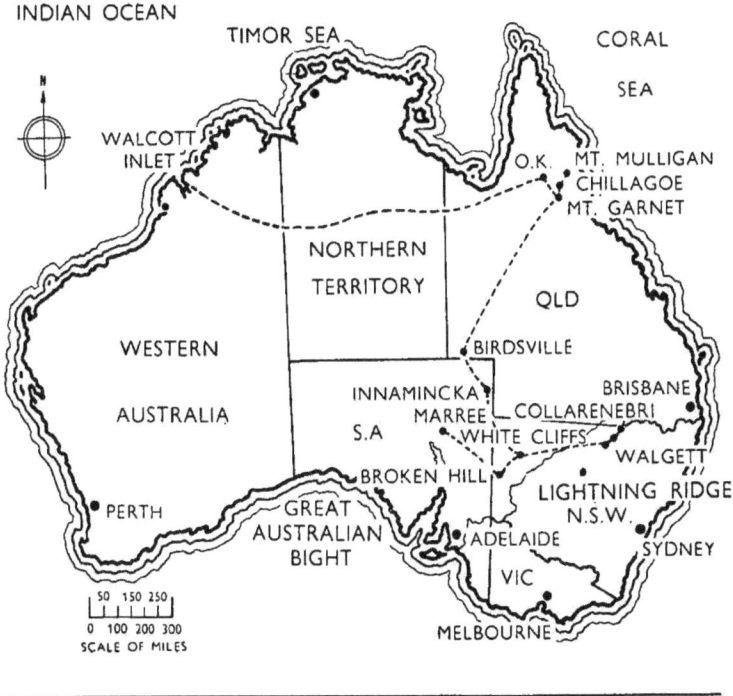

THIS story of Rham Dat, of his good deed, rewarded by the "Fire Stone" years later and nearly two thousand miles to the northward, is a story of what we call coincidence. I doubt if there is any such thing, otherwise all of life would be coincidence. Anyway, the only reason I was now and again to meet Rham Dat and hear of him throughout years in time and over big distances was that we were "following minerals" - he seeking work with the camel-teams carrying goods and ore to and from outlying mineral fields, I wandering from field to field chasing that elusive whisper, "a new rush".

As schoolboys at Broken Hill we got to know the smiling young Afghan Rham Dat, whose first Australian job was with Fezel Dene's camel-team. Often we used to see the teams off as heavy-loaded they lumbered away into the mirages leading to the While Cliffs opal fields, or farther on to Innamincka, to the big stations in the harsh north of South Australia, and to more pleasant lands west of the Darling, farther north still through the Border Gate and on into south-west Queensland.

I left the Silver City for the sea, which wet and salty change soon sent me back to the bush again. I met Rham when humping Matilda from Collarenebri to Walgett, plodding along dreaming of the black opals I hoped to dig from the sandstone hills of Lightning Ridge. Rham Dat with his quick smile had, like me, grown several years older. We said good day by the Namoi, boiled the billy as we yarned about "The Hill", and enjoyed a humble meal under the shade of a mighty river-gum. We waved, "So long! Good luck!" and trudged off, he up river towards Collarenebri, I down river towards Walgett and the track to the Ridge.

It was when gouging on the opal fields we heard how the Afghan had stumbled upon the crippled opal gouger and managed to take him to the Walgett Hospital.

A few years passed, and I was a thousand miles north among the Stannary Hills tin-mines, and yet again met the delighted smile of Rham Dat as he strode ahead of a little camel-team loaded with ore for a noisy battery on the banks of the turbulent Walsh. A bare twelve months later and still farther north, among the copper fumes of then remotest civilization of Chillagoe and Mungana, the Afghan and I met yet again to yarn of friends far away in the Silver City. I happened to mention that the white man he had rescued some years back far away near Walgett had fully recovered and long since returned to Lightning Ridge. It was then that Rham Dat, with great secrecy, showed me his "lucky Fire Stone", and told me the story of the opal. I had long since known of the rescue, of course, but not of the opal. It was a magnificent stone, barred with flashing green and orange over which crimson rolled in waves. When held in a certain way it shimmered as a ball of fire.

I said farewell to the Afghan as, through stunted timber shielding weird outcrops of castellated limestones, he proudly took the lead of a heavily loaded camel-team setting out into a red haze of far northern dust. The country was a choking desolation there just at that time. Rham Dat was in great spirits, a trusted man now of that fine Afghan, Abdul Wade, now sending this pioneer team trudging out towards the pioneers' farthest new horizon, just another horizon. For "out there" O.K. had just been found.

It was on some later trip that Rham Dat, following the tracks of straying camels, became lost in Farthest North. But the end of this story I did not know until years and years later, when yet again I met Rham Dat, three thousand miles west in the Kimberleys.

What a meeting! Over the range towards the wilds of Walcott Inlet, among those tangled valleys and that crazy sea of peaks, the young Afghan and the schoolboy from the Silver City met again.

But now our hair was streaked with silver. What did it matter? Life was still very sweet, and most interesting. Over the campfire that night Rham Dat told me how his lucky Fire Stone had stuck to him and done all for him that the crippled white man had sworn it would, those years agone.

Here is his story.

Rham Dat clutched desperately at a stunted tree with that last frantic strength of the "all in". If he went down now he would never rise again. He was among the foothills of the "Bad Lands", the rocky spurs running from the Dividing Range down into the low-lying wild country of the west coast of Queensland's Cape York Peninsula. Rham Dat did not know this.

He only knew that he had been lost for long, long days.

Never again would he, an Afghan of the Khyber and proud of it, ever imagine he was an Australian bushman. And yet, during the years just gone he had done so well - right up until now. But how different was this vast, empty land to the bush of the camel tracks of Broken Hill and Wilcannia, even of Marree to Port Augusta. How he wished he had never left the brazen lands of those heavily marked tracks now so far, far to the south! Far indeed, for those tracks were away back in other States, in New South Wales and South Australia. And now here he was far north in yet another State, in Queensland - dying of thirst.

"No! No! No!" Rham Dat's bloodshot eyes gazed down at his open hand from which flashed up at him in beautiful colours a magnificent black opal. Rham Dat tried to smile, but his tongue had swollen so the corners of his mouth stretched and cracked.

Leaning there in parched agony, collecting strength for one last desperate effort, the perishing Afghan forced his wandering mind to think of the opal - only the opal!

"Lucky Opal, I cannot die. Lucky Opal, I cannot die." Two days ago he would have bowed to the sandals of Death had it not been for the fearful grip he forced his brain to take of that sentence, he, Rham Dat, who wished so much to live. For the thousandth time he made his possession of the opal come vividly before him. The white man lying there in the dusk with such pain-filled eyes.

Twelve hours stretched there in six inches of water with a broken leg had allowed the water to soak into his body and he was swelling like a poisoned pup.

Rham Dat, accounted one of the strongest of men among the strong camel-men of the West, had lifted the racked body across his shoulder and set off into the raining night. At his first splashing a dingo, quite close, had lifted its head in a howl of baulked longing. Even now his mind shuddered at the recollection of that howl.

Weeks later, in the cool safety of the Walgett hospital ward, the white man had given him the opal.

"It is very lucky, Rham Dat," he had said earnestly, "this stone from the heart of Lightning Ridge: I grew to love it the more I looked at it, it seemed to become part of me. I just could not bring myself to sell it with the others. I've clung to it for five years now and it sure has brought me luck - again and again. Even in this creek. Maybe it was bad luck that my horse shied at the ant-bed and threw me down into the creek with a broken leg. I couldn't have crawled back up that rocky bank, Rham Dat, but I could have crawled out down into deeper water and drowned myself when things seemed hopeless and I grew near mad with the pain. And that blasted dingo gaping down at me. It was then I remembered the lucky opal, snug there in the pouch at my belt. I damn' near prayed to that stone, Rham Dat, never dreamt I'd be so scared to die. The stone is yours now - I promised it you when I heard your horse's hooves coming along up the bank. Believe me, I meant that stone for you if only you could find me and get me away out of it. No! Take it! It is yours! I am superstitious enough to feel that it is yours now, you may need it some time, just as I did. Take it! And now, seal the deal with a promise, your word," he had said most earnestly, "that you will never sell, will never give this opal away unless it be for the price of life itself."

And Rham Dat had given his word.

That had all happened far away in that little hospital at Walgett. It was there that the sick men came from the opal field-when they could get there. And now the opal was quivering in beauty, to the nearly crazy man its dancing colours seemed laughing joyously. This wonderful thing under this blazing sun seemed a living eye of fiery light to the Afghan's beseeching eyes. Answering the trembling of his hand, bands of flame ran over the stone and merged in shimmering waves of orange and green. A fallen drop from God's paint-brush had splashed on the heart of the gem and filled it with sublime rainbows.

Rham Dat imagined he was talking. His cracked lips were moveless, but his fevered brain was praying, "Lucky Opal, Lucky Opal, water, water-water-wa-" A mournful howl rose from the very bushes beside him. Horror stabbed the Afghan's heart. Then it pounded on in a furious tattoo of hope. He lifted up staring, joy-widened eyes to the heavens. By the God of the Afghans, was this not the very howl he had heard on that far night when the crippled white man had wrongly thought his footsteps the sandals of Death?

Two score black figures sprang from the bushes. Rham Dat glared at the animal-like men whose eyes were gleaming with the fever of the hunt.

Sudden joy in his heart, what knew or cared he that these were warriors of the Kulkadoons, killers all? The Lucky Opal had spoken.

He stretched his hand in happy defiance towards the points of the barbed spears and the sun flamed the stone. The eyes of the black men gazed fearfully at this coal of fire which did not burn the hand of their captive.

From the bushes stepped a hunched, shaggy figure with tremendous chest and cavernous black eyes alive with cunning. Round his neck hung a necklace of threaded knuckle-bones of men and women, on his muscular arms gleamed bones which rattled as he walked. He gazed searchingly at the Fire Stone, quivering crimson to the low pulse-beat of the Afghan's hand. The witch-doctor glared up at the Afghan, who, strong man as he was when in health, measured this massive beast's strength as above his own. The animal-like breath from the savage's nostrils carried Rham Dat's mind back to the camel yards of Broken Hill.

The witch-doctor clawed out for the stone but Rham Dat drew his hand back with a warning shake of his head. Instantly spear arms were jerked back and to the click of the woomeras Rham Dat, with wonderful inspiration, held the stone to his forehead and glared threateningly at the witch-doctor. He could see the puzzled indecision in the deep-set eyes as they stared hesitatingly at the eye of fire which burned so angrily in the strange man's forehead. Rham Dat was not in the least afraid. His heart was laughing with a happy song: "Lucky Opal, Lucky Opal, Lucky Opal." Abruptly the witch-doctor turned and strode away through the bushes. Rham Dat, with a flow of new strength -and quickness given to it by a savage spear-jab in the rear-staggered after him.

Rham Dat sat on a rock bathed by sunlight of a Cape York Peninsula morning. Encircling the camp was a grey amphitheatre of granite intersected by gloomy ravines marked by the mouths of caverns among gigantic boulders. High in the blue overhead a flock of waterfowl from the coastal lagoons went sailing past, the beat from their wings com¬ing plainly down to the captive Indian. Longingly he watched their flight-precious flight to freedom.

Except for the laughing yabber of the piccaninnies all Nature was deathly quiet, very still, seemingly the bush was drowsing as if drugged with peace.

But the heart of Rham Dat was very, very sick. Close by a mangy mongrel brought a glistening bone and, dropping in the grass, spread its forepaws upon it and hungrily gnawed. With a mad fury Rham Dat hurled a stone at the mongrel. Never losing its bright new bone, it dived into the long grass, glaring over its shoulder with malice and cunning glinting from its eyes.

Most of the blacks lay sprawled asleep in the warm sun, their bellies much distended. A low, pitiful moaning came from close beside the cooking stones. Rham Dat rose and walked to the twisted black figure. The prisoner's legs had been broken. The tears streamed from Rham Dat's eyes as with his hands he brushed away the meat-ants attacking the man's body. This was the fifth of a string of captives caught three days before, his merciful tum must come that night.

Rham Dat looked to a shaded boulder, then down into the shaggy-browed eyes which spoke up with such unspeakable thanks into his. To move the man as he was would be worse cruelty.

Rham Dat's eyes turned to stare at the witch-doctor watching from his gun yah. Rham Dat lifted the opal to his forehead and glared a defiant threat at the motionless man. Walking determinedly towards the cooking stones, he picked up a blood-spattered nullah then stood over the captive and gazed down with pity and offering in his smile. A great thankfulness flashed over the man's twisted face, his eyes cried with longing, he struggled to raise his head. Rham Dat swung the nullah down.

Rham Dat sat on his granite rock, moving the opal slowly in his hand and noting carefully the angle whence the ball of flame swept over the stone. He was thinking hard. Instinctively he felt that the day had come. For two months now they had held him. Choice food had always been his lot. Rham Dat knew why. They had tried also to teach him their language. Rham Dat knew why. The witch-doctor wanted to learn the secret of the Fire Stone. Though he himself lived on the credulity of others, he was caught by the Flaming Eye. To him Rham Dat was a stranger witch-doctor who owned a charm which Hashed with fiery life that did not burn the owner, and must possess magic powers if he could only find them out.

Rham Dat would have graced the cooking stones long since but that the wizard was afraid of what he did not know about the Wonder Stone. As Rham Dat quickly picked up the language he impressed on the sorcerer the magic of the stone, its uncanny power of causing good and evil, especially evil, and the terrible things that would happen to the man who caused harm to the owner. He had no fear whatever while he held the stone, but immediately it was gone from his possession -

The witch-doctor stood before the Afghan. Around the gunyahs sullen, squatting figures gazed towards the men. Both spoke in the tribal dialect.

"Stranger from the Far Lands, I must have the Fire Eye. My tribe mutter that you are a greater wizard than I, that I fear to kill you for fear of the Magic Eye. This is a lie. I shall kill you now for all the warriors to see if you do not give me the Eye. Give me the Eye-and go!"

"I trust you no more than the snake," sneered Rham Dat, "but I give you the word of a man. Take me to the white man's land. Point out to me a white man's camp. Then I will give you the Fire Eye and go. If you will not - ah, then I shall ask the Eye what happens to you this night."

The superstitious fears of stone-age man quickened within the sorcerer as he gazed half defiantly at the dancing orange and green that blazed in the captive's hand. Muttering a solemn incantation in the Afghan tongue, Rham Dat held the opal to the centre of his forehead, leant forward, and glared into the uncertain eyes of the witch-doctor. Over the opal shot a wave of livid flame, staying there in shimmering bands of red that leapt to the kiss of the sun, a fiery live coal that sent an unknown fear down the witch-doctor's crooked spine.

Rham Dat dropped his hand and stepped threateningly forward.

"The Fiery Eye speaks," he snarled. "Take me now to the white man's land, or this night I shall sit in your gunyah and watch the red-hot cooking stones sizzling into flesh. To your own dog shall I throw your bones. Choose!"

Scowling, the witch-doctor turned towards the waiting camp. With hoarse, beaten voice he shouted for a warrior escort.

And yet again Rham Dat's singing heart blessed the Prophet for the luck of the Lucky Opal.

11

AY-ITA

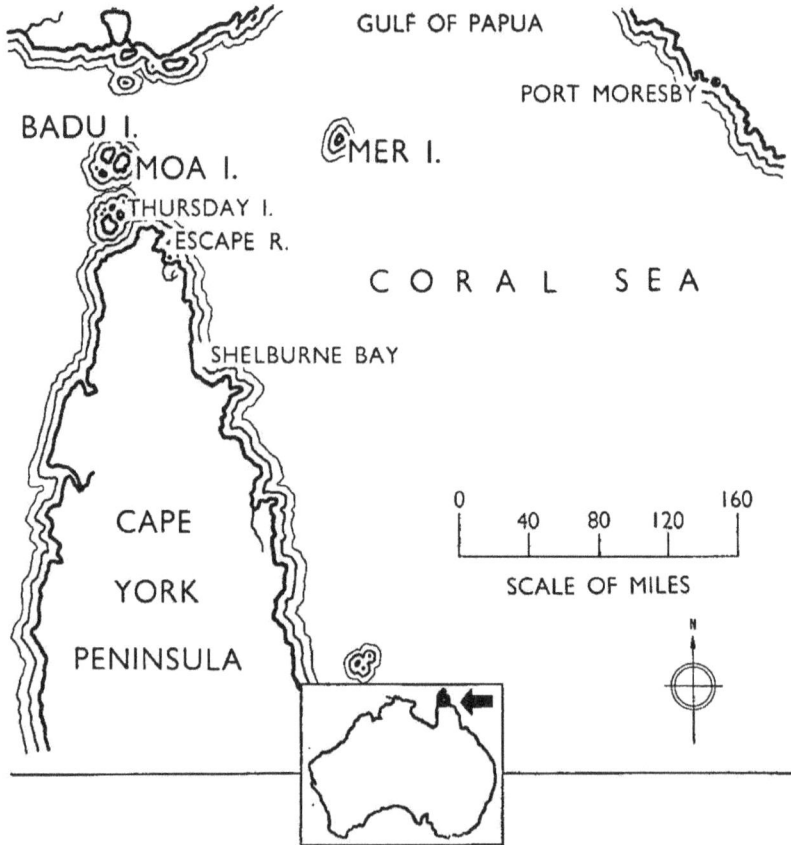

GULF OF PAPUA

PORT MORESBY

BADU I.

MOA I.

MER I.

THURSDAY I.

ESCAPE R.

CORAL SEA

SHELBURNE BAY

CAPE

YORK

PENINSULA

0   40   80   120   160

SCALE OF MILES

N

THE unfolding of this by no means unusual story in the life of an island girl intrigued me very much as a young fellow. Not because all my sympathies were with the girl, but because of the, to me, astonishing cunning-devilry, I believed it to be-of the old sorcerer's mind. That is, when by degrees it was explained to me just what he had done, and why. He could so easily have arranged that Devison should die at sea, in which case all blame would have been upon the girl. But the sorcerer planned for a far more enduring vengeance than this. Then again, it puzzled me exceedingly why the old devil did not later allow it to be made known to Devison, through the crew of the cutter, that it was he, the despised witch-doctor, that had given him that long-continued pain in the belly, and also spoilt his game with the girl. By not doing so, he robbed himself of half his vengeance, it seemed to me.

It was a long time indeed before I realized the full devilry of the sorcerer's revenge. To this day Devison believes the girl gave him that physical and mental agony, followed by a very sore feeling and long-continued mental humiliation.

Otherwise he would have got over it long ago. And the sorcerer then would truly have lost half his vengeance.

Of the sun-kissed delights which pleased the eye on Vala Island none was so sweet as Ay-ita, "Flower of the Morn". The blue of her father's eyes had combined with her mother's bronze skin to fashion Ay-ita's beauty, made adorable by her smile, entrancing through the question in her dancing eyes. Smooth cream her cheeks, flushed with pomegranate under happy excitement. Her grace belied the strength given by seashore life. Yes, to her sea-nymph mother she owed that quick, slim form of fawn-like grace, to her father, alas, her brains-a legacy that bore an inevitable fate.

Ah! If only he had not loved her so much, the daughter he brooded over so. If only - !

So the schooner came and Ay-ita sailed in delight to see the white man's, her father's, country, for he had determined that at least she would learn of her heritage, be able to take her place beside some decent white man he secretly prayed might come some day with love and marriage.

Thus Ay-ita had been educated at that school which has taught so well, but whose teaching has helped ripen other island tragedies-the Thursday Island Convent for Coloured Ladies. And so Ay-ita came to understand the sense of English with the cleverest of Australian girls, while her soft young voice in song left a lingering pleasure to the memory.

She had developed into a beautiful young lady. And then - he died!

And thus the girl came sailing back home to Vala to live among her mother's people, chained by their lives and customs and dream-enshrouded thoughts. The message of the windblown palms, the whispering of the banana leaves, the moonlight on the lonely beach now breathed constantly to her of the white girl's romances far away.

But the planting and digging of taro, the squeals of naked brown children, the canoe song coming with sunset as the men returned from the fishing, these were her daily life, grimly walled in by the sea. In Ay-ita's heart the sea now was cruelly alive, singing its triumph with imprisoning arms crashing against the island's rock-girt walls. Those uncrossable waters barred her from the white people, her father's people, the people of her heart and mind but of only half her blood. Education, having planted knowledge, now left her abandoned to reap the fruit of that which was hers, and yet which was not. Her aching heart rebelled fiercely and alone.

"Thus far but no farther!" her schooling now seemed to have taught.

"Here you cease! Cease! Cease!" murmured the sea. Yes, for such as her just a glimpse within the gate of the white girls' brilliant lives, a taste of life's garden laden with fruit of dreams, then the gate slams, leaving the coloured girl holding her double-edged knowledge, pathetically awed, outside. The body a beautiful shell burning for the wonderful life glimpsed, the brain understanding but caged.

"Just coloured blood!" thought Ay-ita bitterly as she walked the sea-edge seeking shellfish. "Life is a mockery. All it will ever bring me is the existence of a black gin. But for the whites - !"

And she dreamt longingly of the steamers that she had watched sailing into the great white world away from Thursday Island, with happy, ribbon-waving girls aboard-white ones! "I wish the sea had dried," she thought fiercely, "before it brought my father to my mother."

But only Ay-ita's heart cried these thoughts. At the village dances she was the gayest among all the gay young girls, her father's proud blood urged her to be so. She sensed jealousy in the half-veiled taunts of the village girls for her beauty was of white and brown, yet neither one nor the other.

But hardest of all to bear were the desiring eyes, the panther-like body, the grim persistence of Tau-rara, toughest, most reckless diver on the island. Scorning him secretly as a "nigger", she was forced by environment to accept him as an equal. She parried the impulsive man with laughing wit, then sought desperately to hold him back with stinging repartee, while she blessed yet cursed afresh the father who had done this thing only by bitter halves.

During the pearling season luggers from the Coral Sea anchored in the sheltered bay, for these islanders are adept divers and as crew "boys" were in constant demand. But occasionally a lone vessel came sailing in, not seeking a crew-just a white wanderer who while cruising handy to the island had caught the fame of the "Flower of the Morn" and was curious to see for himself. But the sea brought no dream man for her; she answered their rough advances with bitter taunts that left them angrily ashamed.

He came at last, laughing, handsome, a rich man's son from Sydney who cruised the Coral Sea for devilment and pleasure's sake. And Ay-ita's heart beat fast as she smiled him the island welcome on the coral beach.

Devison stared, his blue eyes alight in surprise.

"Holy smoke!" he breathed. "And here it is! An island Cleopatra! By Jove!" His boyish face smiled delightedly.

"You very pretty!" He laughed engagingly. "Eyes alla same stars, lips like him red-fella flower! What name you?"

Ay-ita's lips straightened, the softness melted from the blue eyes. Tossing back a pretty head, she laughed contemptuously.

"I was not educated in the slums," she said clearly, "even though not on the North Shore. We converse in English here."

Turning disdainfully, she walked back to the village, a dignified princess gliding away between the shadowed palms.

Captain Evans guffawed rudely, the Malay mate grinned, the natives grouped around laughed boisterously. Though not understanding, they joyfully sensed Ay-ita had yet again put a white man in his place.

Now Devison was an over-petted son and had bullied his own spoilt way too long through life. That natives should laugh at his expense made him furious. But it was through his own ignorance that of them all it should be Rohurara he pushed contemptuously aside as he stepped back into the dinghy - a thing he should never have done. Not because Rohurara was withered and bent - Devison would not have cared had the old scarecrow been a young giant - but because he was a famed witch-doctor, a real one. But then, Devison did not understand witch-doctors. If their powers had been explained to him he would have laughed in scornful contempt. Amid an ominous silence he pulled himself back to the cutter, and he could handle an oar.

But Ay-ita's heart was singing with joy, tinged with triumph. She knew her rebuke had struck more effectively than coy glances and words could ever have done.

Devison wooed Ay-ita with all the practised graces of a city jazz-sheikh, then put the best drawing-room manners and the fast-failing memory of his college poetry into it. Piqued by only partial success, he put all he had into it - his big, bullying figure that looked so well in swimming togs, his handsome face with that "you're the only one for me" smile, his dashing ways that could so swiftly change to wheedling-and in amazed surprise was forced to fall back on what brains he had. It was a game that tingled the blood and warmed the heart, an entrancing game in the seductive quiet of the beach under shadowed palms in flower-scented air, with the croon of the sea lullaby to banish thoughts of the far-away world.

Not that Devison cared a hang about the outside world; it was his to go to when he wanted to. Meanwhile, what a throbbing prize to cap the holiday of a lifetime! With eager hand he fondled the rich tresses framing the face endearingly close to his.

"Your hair is perfumed like the crushed hearts of roses, Ay-ita," he whispered hotly. "In its clinging strands I steal to a garden of dreams where my heart has flowered for you. Your eyes - oh, Ay-ita! - your eyes are pools of wonder that bathe my love for you."

And Ay-ita, trembling with the joy of her lips against his would close her eyes and think very, very hard of her white father until with his ghostly presence came strength to hold the wild man back lest she forget all she had been taught.

And Tau-rara the diver, crouching in the shadows, would grind his teeth and wait, knowing his safest bulwark was the girl herself. Her white blood would finally give her to him. For Rohurara the sorcerer had told him so, had assured him it would be so-and advised him not to strike, but to bide his time. Thus he dared not take her-yet.

But how hard it was to watch and wait!

Devison now waited also, but very differently. The citadel was so slowly but so surely weakening he felt delight in toying with the joys of desire. Just a little longer. He still had two months' holiday cruise left. He would dally here, of course. Then a fortnight later he registered his second shock. Storming the citadel with such mad, hot words of love that he dimly wondered if it really could be himself uttering them, he was taken aback when the white-faced girl with the veins blue in the closed eyelids whispered faintly of marriage.

It was Devison's shocked surprise that really saved the girl. Her swimming blue eyes opened understandingly, to slowly gleam with a heart's resolve.

Devison promised anything, everything. And the girl smiled through tears of joy. Then Devison quickly found that promises were accepted only as deeds! His wits travelling on the wings of passion, he promised immediate marriage - the marriage of her people, now, this very evening!

And cold fear clutched Ay-ita's heart, though her sweet face smiled. For Devison, his third shock. She wished to be married at Thursday Island among the friends of her schooldays-or at the very least by the missionary on Damley Island.

"But - but -" stuttered Devison, "we will be married according to the native custom. It is quite right! Why, it is the way your father married!"

Something stabbed Ay-ita's heart. "But the world has changed," she whispered. "In those days the native custom was all that mattered. In these days - you understand?"

Devison understood, only he did not want to understand. So alone he rowed back to the cutter, and the rowlocks croaked his bitter disappointment.

Devison fought hard for the girl in the month that followed. He grinned morosely at the thought that if only he put the same amount of feverish energy into his father's business he would rear that edifice to the skies. And kill the old man with shock.

The girl fought desperately now. Her mother's blood cried, "Give! Give! Give!" The white father's spirit face warned, "Hold! Hold! Hold!" Ay-ita wept and prayed that she might win in the end. She would possess this man by the power of her beauty and mind and love. He could not resist much longer. Ay-ita prayed to the white man's God for this one great chance to live a white girl's life.

An evening came when he told her harshly, "I come for the last time tomorrow evening, Ay-ita, then with the dawn breeze I sail. My holiday is finished. Tomorrow evening, if you are ready, I marry you here among your people. We will sail for Brisbane. If you still say no, then tomorrow evening, for the last time of all, I will bid you good-bye." He stepped into the dinghy and pushed angrily off.

Devison had no intention of leaving the island without the girl. The desire for her clung to him day and night, her presence floated out to him with every breath of the sea; he could not let go. But he meant to possess her without being tied. He had reasoned it out as a contest inevitably meaning in the end spoils to the victor. He smiled grimly, while marvelling at the strength that was hers.

Ay-ita, forlorn on the beach, cried softly into the darkness. The fading dinghy seemed pulling away her very heart. The reaction from the passionately tense moments of the weeks gone by dragged her irresistibly back to her people.

Her sobs quietened as the white father's face faded into the leering brown one of old Rohurara, the witch-doctor. A thrill of hope warmed her fear, memories of miracles whispered in the village homes brought hope to her heart. She stared guiltily along the beach, frightened at the brooding silence of the night. Dormant superstitions rapidly awaking, she crept fearfully towards Rohurara's gloomy hut.

Poor Ay-ita! Under the dire distress of her white blood the superstitions of the brown were struggling painfully for mastery.

Rohurara, the feared one, did not stir as the girl stood before him.

"Rohurara!" she whispered and gasped the native salu¬tation of respect that had never passed her lips before. She dared not glance at the ominous charms hanging from the smoke-blackened walls; with cold fear at her heart she stared down at this withered hump of skin and bones that was her last faith in life.

Rohurara spoke. In that strained silence it seemed like a thin, cracked voice whispering from some other world.

"Ay-ita has come for a charm to hold the love of the white man!"

Ay-ita's trembling fingers reached her heart. "Speak!" commanded Rohurara harshly.

"It is so," she whispered.

After brooding moments Rohurara spoke again.

"I will give you a charm that will make the white man's thoughts be of you for many moons, that will make your face be burnt into his brain as with pains of fire. He will never, never, never forget Ay-ita. Will that do?"

"Yes," she breathed.

From between crooked feet he handed her a powder twisted in banana-leaf.

"Choose two young coconuts as the sun sinks tomorrow," he ordered. "Put this within the milk of the one. When he comes coax him to drink the milk, you drink of the other. Do not delay the play, otherwise he will be too angry to drink when he bids you good night. Do as I say, and he will never forget Ay-ita. Never!"

The girl stole from the hut, her heart beating a tattoo of triumph. And that evening came-bringing Devison hot with desire. Gaily Ay-ita challenged him to plight their troth in the milk of the young coconut. And Devison drank. But when he claimed her Ay-ita steadfastly refused.

Devison called a furious good-bye from the beach. "It is the last, the very last! When dawn breaks I sail, never to return. If still you would come, canoe out before the morning breeze. If not, then do not wave my sail away, for I will not wish to see you." And he splashed savage oars into the water.

Ay-ita gazed across the bay from tear-dimmed eyes, a quivering smile of hope and fear making her face beautiful.

He could not forget her, for he had drunk of the coconut milk. The very spirits of her people breathed he could never, never forget her. He would not sail at dawn.

Dawn broke with a Hush to the east, bringing a whispering breeze. Ay-ita stretched her cream-white aims towards the cutter, eyes alight with triumph as her heart crooned intense thanks to her native gods.

The cutter had not sailed!

Devison, lying wrapped in the black sulks, was cursing at the fate that had played him this false move, blissfully unaware that something was about to happen that would drive all thoughts of love from his mind for a long, cruel time.

His futile anger ceased as he clasped a wondering hand to his stomach. Soon he was in agony. He rolled from the bunk, screaming to the crew, "Up sail - sail for a doctor!"

A frightened boy hurried to him with a bucket of seawater. Devison drank in an agonized hope. But Rohurara was no bungler. As the boat gathered way Devison prayed for Thursday Island hospital - would moan his prayers for many, many long hours to come.

Yes! All his life he would remember Ay-ita-but not one thought of Rohurara the insulted witch-doctor.

As the cutter's broad mainsail rattled noisily up the girl's flushed cheeks drained white. The old, icy fear clutched her heart.

Unbelieving, she gazed. Oh, the white man's God! Yes!

So clearly came the rattle of the pulley blocks, the rumble of the anchor chain. Oh, God - the native's god! The anchor was now off bottom - the mainsail was filling - the cutter forging ahead.

Black bodies hauled fast at the tackle. A rippling line of foam frothed back from the graceful bows. She became a thing of life with cordage humming to the sail-kissed breeze.

Ay-ita raced along the beach screaming, "Oh, wait! Wait! Wait! Oh, take me with all my heart!"

And then Tau-rara the diver grasped her arm.

12

THE UNKNOWN QUANTITY

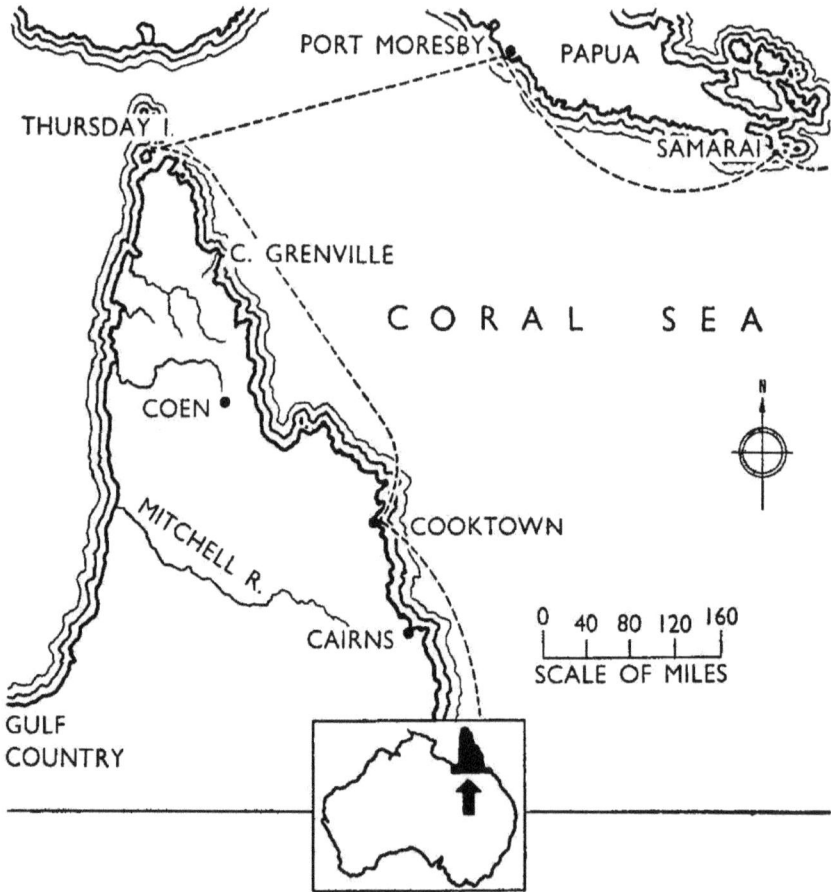

THE "essence" of this strange happening came to me but in fragments, I might say, almost in whispered fragments, and through coincidence of time and environment. I have tried to join these elusive wisps of story together into a pattern of what certainly appears to have actually happened.

Peaceful the sea, night dreamily humming to the ship's vibrations. Three men lazing back upon easy chairs on deck, too contented even to be smoking, not even thinking, though thought was drifting through their minds with a magical ease.

"I hate breaking the silence," exclaimed Collins, "but I feel compelled. If a man could always draw his thoughts from the unexplainable depths that I feel now he'd solve the impossible, maybe the secret of life itself. Are you two slaves to the same enchantment, or is it that the Coral Sea has entranced me?"

"I feel as if I was a sponge of contentment," replied Lincoln in drawling voice, "absorbing thought through no effort of my own. So unusual, most pleasantly so. If this atmosphere were only chronic I'd never leave the tropics. Some spirit of this mysterious night seems controlling whatever is *me,* and I'm just floating along. I suppose the mundane reason is that we three tired businessmen are under the spell of some combination of conditions that makes our minds completely relaxed at this moment."

"Good meals, no women, mind contented," grunted Burke.

"H'm," mused Collins. "My mind doesn't respond to such agreeable specifications, worse luck, excepting at this precise moment. However, as our thoughts appear in such harmony I'm tempted to test the riddle a little further. Now, right at this second I am irresistibly impressed by the apparent presence of that strange fellow - Larvey!"

Burke leant abruptly forward. "*He* seems to be urging me come down below!" he spoke almost agitatedly. "The pull of some mental magnet that seems to be compelling obedience, is the only way I can explain the feeling. Strange - and decidedly uncomfortable!"

Lincoln stood up. "I've taken the line of least resistance - since wedlock," he smiled and walked towards the companion-way. His friends followed him down the brightly lit stairs and into the cabin passage-way.

Larvey stood erect in a blaze of electric light, a queerly satisfied smile curling his lips as they approached. Something in those hazel eyes compelled the new-comers to gaze at his smooth, untroubled face. Beside him stood a man as if entranced, his frightened eyes widening in mute appeal as the three men now stood by.

Larvey just looked at the man-looked into him. Speechlessly, the man gazed back. Then hesitantly he drew a revolver, his temple veins swelling as he pointed the weapon to his heart, his eyes now staring in frantic appeal.

The three men leaned forward - remained helplessly thus. Their mouths opened in amazed protest-remained open - speechless.

A report, clang of metal, thud of falling body, fumes of gunpowder. The men rushed forward and bent over him. The third mate appeared from nowhere, two stewards came hurriedly.

Larvey shrugged to the mate's question. "He simply walked from the cabin complaining that he was sick of life - and shot himself through the heart. I tried to stop him, but he was too quick. These gentlemen witnessed the tragic occurrence."

Lincoln lowered the dead man's head and sprang up.

"You - you say exactly what happened! I saw it all!"

Burke pushed his excited face before the mate. "I saw it!" he stuttered. "I s-saw this man-s-saw him-try to save this poor wretch -" Burke's voice trembled to silence.

"But," shouted Collins, "but he was too late! I saw - I saw it all!"

Well-disciplined stewards bundled the body into the cabin while others hurried about cleaning up. Curious passengers were dispersed.

"Come with me to the captain's cabin," ordered the mate.

And there the witnesses exactly repeated their statements. Larvey was quite calm, the witnesses nervily excited in emphasizing what they had told the mate. A case of deliberate suicide.

Several hours later the three sat in Burke's cabin. Conspirators in the condemned cell could not have appeared more nerve-strained.

"What is the explanation?" whispered Collins tragically. "We cannot control our own speech!"

"Worse!" replied Burke hoarsely. "Far worse. We make speech deliberately lie against truth, and every decent feeling in our nature!"

"It wasn't hypnotism," whispered Lincoln. "I am familiar with that subject. *He* was enslaved by some frightful form of mind control as, Heaven help us, we ourselves still are. We have the most vivid recollection of what occurred and yet we cannot relate the fact even among ourselves. It is like being locked in an asylum while knowing oneself most agonizedly sane. Heavens, what *shall* we do?"

Only the vibrating silence on shipboard after midnight replied.

In his cabin sat Larvey as if unconscious of this world while listening for some phantom whisper from another. And, now smiling triumphantly, relaxing with all the lithe grace of a cat, the smile fading to an expression of utter repose, the fine eyes froze slightly as they gazed straight through the ship. Such quietness in the cabin that the crackle as a cockroach scuttled over paper sounded loud and clear.

Smaller than the palm of a man's hand, a faint mist formed before Larvey's gaze. It spread like the gathering of tremulous wisps of spider-web, a phantom sheet that might vanish at a breath, its edges floating in air.

Within this screen of intense thought came shadows building up into forms of men growing plainer as if wisps of thought were melting into threads weaving a pattern, then form, then faces and drawn expressions and agonized eyes. And in Larvey's consciousness there whispered voices, faint yet distinct, like telephone voices coming from far, far away.

Collins was leaning with a tremulous questioning towards his friends.

"If we can't speak of what we actually saw, at least we can write it!"

Quick relief shone from the listeners' faces. Burke thrust a writing pad on the table. Collins bent over it, pen in hand, fingers trembling with eagerness. He hesitated a moment, almost as if listening. Then he wrote easily, unhesitatingly.

The pen scratched to a stop. Collins stared unbelievingly, broken-hearted, at the writing: "I endorse every word Larvey said. He did his best to stop the suicide but was not in time - J. H. Collins."

Slowly he tore the leaf out and handed it to Burke. "See what you write," he whispered hoarsely.

And Burke wrote: "It was a simple case of suicide.

Larvey was just too late to save the man. - L. F. Burke."

Burke wrote again. He tried the third time, writing quite easily and naturally, his face growing frantic as his fingers formed words opposite in sense to those his mind dictated.

Lincoln took the pen, but flung it down with a sentence half finished. "It's no use!" he almost sobbed. "I *cannot* write the words my mind dictates. We're like a ship without a compass - men without minds! What shall we do!"

In the stillness within his cabin Larvey smiled his uncanny triumph. Slowly the mist faded, the forms disolved. He sighed, breathed deeply, then rose and stretched luxuriously.

Collins started warningly at the knock on the cabin door.

His companions stared. *Something* told them.

Larvey softly closed the door behind him, smiling a moment as a father might regard his rebellious children.

"I feel an explanation is owing to you gentlemen," he said gently. "You shall have it - because it amuses me. You saw me, for good reasons of my own, induce the late deceased to depart this life. You witnessed that incident because I willed you to come and see. I may add also that the manipulation of the minds of you three men provided the spice in the culmination of a very interesting little experiment. You will admit that I have not, as you would term it, slipped.

"And now you find that you are mentally enchained by a will-power far superior to your own," he proceeded. "You will continue to be bound by my will thus, simply because a quality, a mental defence in your fathers' fathers' minds became atrophied through disuse as Humanity strode on into this darkening mental age of materialistic evolution.

"However, a few, a very, very few of us have retained and nourished this power from the priceless knowledge of the ancients. In a minor way, I have proved this to you. However, the undreamt of powers latent in the human mind are quite beyond the understanding of such as you in this 'civilized age'. For you have not the time to think. Suffice to say, you have been compelled to witness a happening which according to your ethics represents murder. Again, you find you cannot speak about what you saw, worse still, when you try you say the exact opposite to what your whole being is crying out to declare.

"Yet again, you find you cannot even write of what you saw, that your pen is traitor to your mind and stronger than your physical power and will. By no means whatsoever can you now, or ever will, impress upon your fellow men what actually occurred.

"And now - farewell! Occasionally I shall think of you three with amusement, and at odd times as diversion I will bring my presence to you, merely for practice, though my material body may be a thousand miles away. In all other things you will be 'normal', so there is no need to worry over our successful experiment. And now, thanking you for your attentive hearing, I wish you good night and good-bye!

Such is the difficult story, as I have tried to piece together what seems to have happened. And now, you must try to work it out for yourself. None of those who actually took part in the incident told me about it; they couldn't, if the story is true. It was told me, long afterwards, by another passenger on that ship. To use his own words: "I swear I was there, Jack, and heard and saw every bit of the happening. But I was present in a dream. Think me silly if you want to, but I was *there!* My body was sound asleep in another cabin. But whatever is the Me in me was there floating about throughout that ship wherever the actors in that drama were. I saw everything - heard everything. And now you can work it out for yourself, for it is beyond me."

So there you are. He swears he was a witness, but a *phantom* witness. To have made accusations based on things allegedly seen and heard in his sleep would have been futile in face of what appeared a straight-out suicide, backed up by four very wide-awake witnesses. who were certainly present in the flesh. Anyway, he was too bewildered to say anything at the time, too startled to believe his own self.

So, there is the complete story - to me, much more interesting now than when I first heard it, in view of "modern" discoveries concerning that perhaps most wonderful subject in the world, the mind of man.

What fantastic powers and possibilities dwell in the mind of man we are only now beginning to discover. So far as this strange story is concerned, perhaps that sleeper *did* see, *did* hear. His "dream mind", while his body was asleep, may have "tuned in" to the mesmerist's mind and to the agitated, hypnotized minds of the others. The human "radiations", all necessary (and at present only guessed at) conditions may have been suitable, and in that dream state his mind mingled with those of the others, so he quite possibly did see and hear.

What would be *your* explanation?

13

THE CURSE

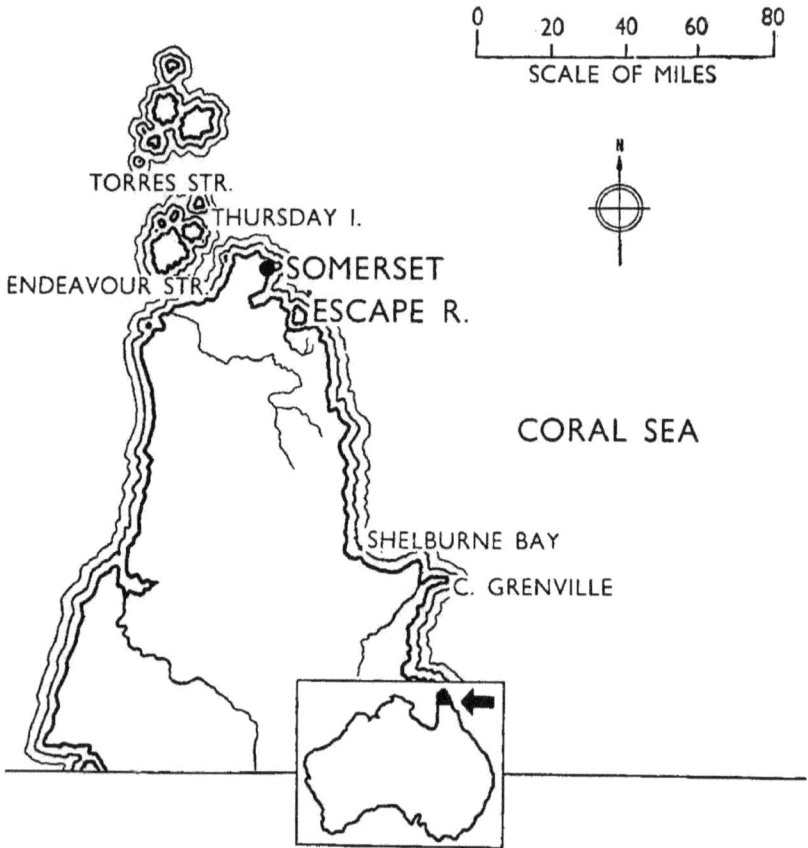

I FIRST heard this story when anchored within the broad mouth of that practically unknown river, the Escape. A weird place, hiding itself away both by land and sea. The outlet is apparently blocked by Turtle Head Island, which is merely a huge rock somewhat resembling a turtle's head, apparently maliciously thrown down by some giant hand from the sky to block all sign of river from the sea, while preventing anything in the river from escaping out to sea. Hemmed in by low, scrubby ridges on its northward side, the southern bank is a maze of mangroves intersected by dank, twisty waterways nearly hidden by dwarfed vegetation, with farther back that frightful turkey-bush scrub almost encroaching upon swamps of the pitcher plant, the meat-eater, whose flower traps and digests insects.

The aborigines, comparatively plentiful in my day in the Peninsula, roamed from the Fingerpoint (Peak Point and Cape York) the twenty odd miles down to the northern bank of the Escape, but shunned the tangled fastnesses of the southern. All manner of devils and evil spirits browsed among those morasses, they declared, and told grim tales to prove it. Besides, it was the home of the Wirrinu, those fiercely vengeful protectors of the Wirrininni. These latter were the "little mens", a tribe of tiny dwarfs. This was merely a fairy story, I am sure, though I suppose it could have had some factual origin in the ages of long ago. Anyway, in my youthful curiosity I never even saw the track of one. The aborigines laughed when I said this, and declared I could stand beside a hundred of them in that sea of plant life and would not see one - which sounded creepily probable. They further assured me that I, or any clumsy non-seeing white man, could practically tread upon one of the wee, bearded warriors and he could thrust his tiny poisoned spear into me and vanish before the yell was out of my throat. That did not sound too good, either.

It was on the southern bank, within a hundred yards of our anchorage, that poor Kennedy, stumbling onward in dogged misery, was speared, actually within sight, if he could have crossed over and climbed the ridge on the northern bank, of the government relief schooner *Ariel* awaiting him in that bay just over the ridge. It was the Escape River, too - if this queer, unpredictable waterway could be called a real river - which gave those successful explorers the Jardine boys their last troubles when, at exhaustion point, they sought again and again to cross its maze of entangling swamps. The boys, too, like the ill-fated Kennedy, were within cooee of journey's end.

I first saw that river in company with "Beetles" Jardine, son of Frank the explorer. There were still natives about who had known the old man and the last hectic days of Somerset, It is fascinating to be camped in such places and listen to the stories of historical events from the actual actors, or those closely connected with them.

So it was there, in Australia's farthest north, anchored in the mouth of that lonely, uninhabited river, that I listened to the story of Hammond the diver, and the curse of Curra-murra the witch-doctor. The natives at low tide took me by canoe to near the river-mouth and, with awed tones and gestures, pointed down to the dim shapes of the boulders under water where the sorcerer had "planted" the girl to trap his enemy the white diver.

Later on, on Thursday Island, I heard that the diver had "drunk himself crazy", but, knowing the story from the natives on the Escape, I believe it was the dreadful experience that actually drove the man crazy.

Judge for yourself.

"I call on the Spirit of the Great One! Yea, white man, may you die a hundred deaths and yet live to die again, under the water and beneath the stars and in the long, lonely nights within the gunyahs of your people. May the sea when it dreams haunt your mind with the terrors of its depths! May the night breezes moan with accusing voices, may the stars seek you out wherever you may hide and their misty twinkling be the tearful eyes of those you have wronged. I call on the Great Spirit whose name we dare not whisper, to bear me out in my righteous curse. I, Curra-murra, have spoken!"

A frightened silence cloaked the lugger, intensified by the panting of the witch-doctor's breath. His trembling arm accused Hammond, who frowned upon this savage that dared beard him aboard his own ship. The sorcerer's bloodshot eyes were aflame within their shaggy sockets, the naked body offended with its stench of human oil.

As Hammond sprang below, the witch-doctor pivoted on his heels and dived overboard. And the crew did not, or would not, see his head rise to the surface.

The lugger lay at anchor just within the broad mouth of the Escape River, on the wild east coast of Cape York Peninsula. The sunlight of far northern Queensland bathed the wooded hills and made all things pleasant.

Presently there fluted across the water the triumphant call of a black drongo. As one man, the native crew sighed. Reluctantly Hammond carried his rifle below. Hushed whispers broke out among the crew.

Hammond was worried. Business worries. And shell promised to be low-priced again this season. As an added handicap, Curra-murra had chosen this chance to settle a score. Hammond well knew that now his native crew would work but sulkily, they would be anxious to escape a boat cursed by the dreaded witch-doctor.

He frowned at the untidy cabin. Tall and brown of face he was a handsome man, but the chisels of worry were working at the corners of his eyes.

Mechanically he reached for his pipe. There would be no hope of getting a tap of work out of the superstitious crew today. After all, he could not blame Curra-murra, His enmity was natural. Hammond wished now that he had not been such a fool as to get even with the cunning nigger when he had to return and work in the man's own tribal country.

It was natural that Curra-murra should influence the young Omen of his tribe not to go to sea in the white men's ships. Once they were aboard the shelling luggers the witch-doctor's hold on them was weakened, each day of "civilization" loosened it more and more. Year by year he saw his tribesmen vanishing under the influence of the white people as salt vanishes when washed away by the river. And the heart of Curra-murra was sore.

But the shell fleets must have crews. Hammond thought glumly of the money and time expended before his own lugger was manned, and ill-manned at that.

Ah well, he had got even by playing Curra-murra off against the mission people. He had used them to take away Mena and Weinapa to the mission, far out of reach of Curra-murra. They were only girls of seven and eight, but in another three years they would have been the old devil's wives. He had a mortgage on the pick of the young lubras from babyhood, but Hammond had cheated him out of two, anyway. The mission would see to that.

But Hammond soon afterwards had been made to realize that now it would be almost impossible to secure recruits from these tribes under Curra-murra's control. In desperation he had tried to appease the influential sorcerer by giving him Alberta.

Hammond clenched his pipe. Damn Alberta and those trusting brown eyes of hers! She had worried him more than all else combined. Not a straight-out worry. Worse - an elusive accusation that tormented his mind day and night, a persistent whispering that he had done a wrong past forgiveness - past anything.

Curra-murra was not in the least propitiated by the sacrifice. Hammond's heart whispered that the sacrifice was not his, he had conveniently got rid of Alberta because he had tired of her. And Curra-murra should have been delighted.

For Alberta, though a coloured girl, was nearly white in skin and soul - but what did Curra-murra know of the soul! - her father an educated Chinese, her mother three-quarters white.

Quaintly pretty, with her lithe little figure she had once been beautiful to the white man's view. She spoke a lisping English, laughed with a white girl's happiness; her ways were dainty, she dressed like a white girl - and the black man's dream of paradise is a white girl.

But Curra-murra had not responded. The old devil was too vindictively clever.

Night came, and the world dreamed - except those inhabitants that prey by night. And the bosom of night seemed, as it always seems, to harbour more things by night than day in that weird country fringing the mouth of the Escape. Fishes that flurried the depths with rush of phosphorescent foam, the subdued cough of a crocodile, the whistle of unseen wings, two fiery marbles where a fang-toothed animal scouted, a creaking amongst the mud-slimed mangrove roots that might be anything, strange sounds upon the beaches and mud flats and forest lands, and - yes, men of the night, but no sound betrayed them and, being black, their naked forms were dissolved in the night.

As for the peaceful things, there twinkled a haze of stars when the scuds passed, an elusive tang of air-borne blossoms, the lugger dim-shaped in midstream, a wary sleeping of wild things among the trees and cavern rocks.

The crew slept. Being afraid that night, they snored below decks with the cockroaches scuttling over them nibbling their thick, horn-like toenails. Hammond half dreamed in the cabin, with an uneasy subconsciousness of some intangible presence close by, something indefinitely near, whispering him, calling persistently, a presence that once had been sweet and desirable to be near, but now -

Happy morning came, bringing a thankful awakening and breakfast and active life. Hammond finished his smoke while the crew, in sulky fashion, prepared the diving gear.

The red cliffs dominating the river-mouth flamed like molten copper as the sun leapt from the sea. The wide water rested tranquilly with upon it that listening quietness which is part of the spell of the tropics. The vibrant, flute-like call of a black drongo trilled from bank to bank. The crew, from beneath shaggy brows, sneaked a quick glance at the morose white master. The bar at the river-mouth was musically noisy. Inside, where the lugger lay, was deep water.

The Escape carries an inner channel of considerable depth. Some of the finest pearl-shell from the Barrier has been fished there. But it is seldom worked because it is a hunting-ground of the tiger shark, the sea-going crocodile, the monstrous diamond fish and the giant groper. The native diver dreads the place and even the suit-diver gives it a wide berth. So many demons in the one locality would frighten most men.

Hammond's face as he stared unseeing into the water bespoke nerves. But he was not worrying about what might be waiting deep down where soon he must go, for he counted on the Escape giving him a rich haul of shell and ease from financial troubles. Nor of the sore fact that since the Japanese had come in force to Thursday Island the white diver was being driven fast from his own Barrier seas. No, he was not worrying about these things.

But he sensed an unreasoning dread of going below this morning. And an equally unexplainable force was urging him down, down-

Abruptly he turned to the diving gear. Silently they helped him prepare, clumsily he stepped overside and clung to the little ladder, lastly and apparently gladly they screwed on his face-glass. The tender stood by his work, two boys stood by the pump handles, Hammond like a clumsy monster let go the ladder and slowly sank. Pretty bubbles marked his going, and then the water quietened.

Hammond came to rest upon a gravelly bottom. He stood awhile, adjusting the air-valve until he had just the correct pressure of air pouring into the suit. Like the heart-beats of a sleeping giant he could hear the air-pump up above on the lugger's deck. All else was oppressive silence and the feeling that long experience had never tided him over, that all his earth life was compressed in the air within his suit, just a layer of air and a film of rubber between him and a world fiercely, overwhelmingly antagonistic to man. Such a feeling is near enough to the truth, and is helped by the fact that when a man is down there, strained by water pressure and compressed air, the human mind is apt to leap to vivid imaginings between the borderland of life and death. Hammond often secretly congratulated himself that his own particular "under-water feeling" was at least eminently sane. Cumbrously he walked ahead. The going just there was easy, a gravel patch clear of boulders and marine growths and holes. The tide had not yet quite turned. Presently he would feel its power like a solidly moving wall pushing against him, and then he must move *with* it.

As he lumbered on he searched the bottom, eyes alert from behind the face-glass of the ugly helmet.

For although the pearly oyster is often large enough to weigh six pounds, still the jealous sea camouflages her pearls as mother earth hides her gold. The shell is indistinguishable, for it merges into any particular background the sea spreads for it. But the oyster must eat and thus open its shell just a little, and this little exposes the mother-of-pear] lining on the lip of the shell and the glint of its betraying beauty catches the diver's eye. Uncannily aware of the stranger's presence, often yards away, the big oyster closes its shell with a peculiar movement which also attracts the wonderful eye of that sublimely developed animal, man.

Once noted, he must not for an instant take his eye off the position of the shell, otherwise he is lucky indeed if he can again find it so cunningly wedged in amongst the ferns and Bowers, the shells and coral growths, the brilliantly hued "vegetable gardens" upon whichever portion of the ocean bed he is searching.

Presently through the green twilight there loomed fantastic shapes of boulders. Hammond made towards them, careful that his air and

Presently through the green twilight there loomed fantastic shapes of boulders. Hammond made towards them, careful that his air and safety lines did not become entangled when he trod between those shadowy, bulky sides. Careful of holes in the sea Boor, also cautious as he lab-oriously stepped over or edged round the smaller stones while his trained mind warned against venturing too far in amongst the boulders looming taller than a man, their bulk and the crevices between them so deceptive. A false step and, should the tide tum strongly and quickly, he might easily be jammed fast.

Here and there were luxuriant rockeries of orchid-like and ferny growth unequalled in fantasy and beauty by any garden on earth. Hammond gazed a moment, his thoughts unaccountably, perilously wavering on earth life. He noticed, though, that those plants possessing long stems were now standing upright, their feathery tops seductively waving towards him. That meant the tide was just on the turn!

He hesitated. To be perfectly safe, he should tum back to the open stream now. But a compelling force urged him farther in, some vital principle strong as the growing tide that would presently bend these stemlike Bowers and things far stronger as it pushed irresistibly onward to its end. But this force urging Hammond was a mind force and its strength, like that of the tide, unseen and all compelling.

Perhaps it was his lucky day! There might be a pearl of pearls awaiting him amongst these tomblike rocks. It was a likely-looking place, and he so badly needed a pearl. He would venture just a little farther. A clump of white "lilies" clinging to a boulder, eerie in their sea beauty, swayed tide-kissed towards him as if beckoning. He crept on.

Hammond sighed as if his heart had broken - and lost control of his mind, that control so delicately balanced when a man is working deep down below. Alberta stood before him in naked loveliness, bathed in that soft green twilight of just below the sea surface. Shadowing her was a flat-topped rock, her hair floating just above its crown. Hammond remembered how proud she was of her hair, and now it softly waved about her like wispy masses of sea-silk fondled by the tide. She gazed with appealing eyes and lips that were crying.

He could not hear her voice, or even the throb of the pumps; he heard nothing, but sensed an indefinite something between himself and Alberta preventing him from going to her; she was so near and yet they were in different worlds, and yet both together, while something fiercely whispered that they would never be together again, never in physical life.

An undersea current swept the rock and twisted the girl completely round. Hammond crouched down before she swayed facing him again, his brain clamouring to hold on to sanity.

For this was a dead girl! She was not alive at all, he was at the bottom of the sea amongst towering rocks, and the tide had turned. And Alberta's back was all eaten away.

How stiff were her rounded breasts! And how swollen the ankles where a thong of native bark lashed them to a stone! This was Curra-murra's work.

Sick with fear and fury, Hammond struggled upright.

He wanted fiercely to shoot Curra-murra and then - himself.

For he was really responsible. Alberta's life was a life equal to his. By what right had he taken it? Though her skin was coloured that made no difference. How olive- white her skin was now! How her eyes stared! Why, she had been educated at the Thursday Island Convent, she could play the violin and sing and dance and laugh with the joy of life; she loved pretty dresses and-she loved him. And he had given her to a blacks' camp to live the life of a gin, less thought of than the dogs. Curra-murra had been less cruel!

Oh God! For the girl swayed forward, her arms gently floated open. Hammond's mind calmed, suddenly. He grimaced. At this rate he would soon be raving mad; air and water pressure would hasten that. But he would keep calm just a little while, for the witch-doctor's curse trembled in his mind. "May you die a hundred deaths and yet live to die again, under the water and beneath the stars and in the long, lonely nights within the gunyahs of your people."

Ah well, he had already died one underwater death.

He would die just once more, easily this time and of his own will; he owed it to Alberta not to leave her again. A life for a life-and he would cheat Curra-murra of those other deaths!

He stood there waiting while the tide strengthened and the girl's frizzy hair played round her ears. His heart warmed, for her face seemed losing its pathetic loneliness. A curling sea frond reached out with the tide and caressed her body and Hammond smiled back. He braced himself, for he felt a giant hand against his chest. Serenely he awaited the increasing strength of the tide.

And then Hammond died again as there half Heated, half swam down to settle on the flat-topped rock a monstrous shape of knobby body and squat legs armed with claws. A hideous snout poked out over the girl's shoulder and Hammond gazed into fiendish eyes deep-set in horny sockets, slits threatening unmentionable things to this apparent robber of its prey.

Hammond's mind became panic-stricken, instinct alone guided his body in the quick flight. Trembling fingers screwed tight the air-escape valve

14

THE TOM-TOM

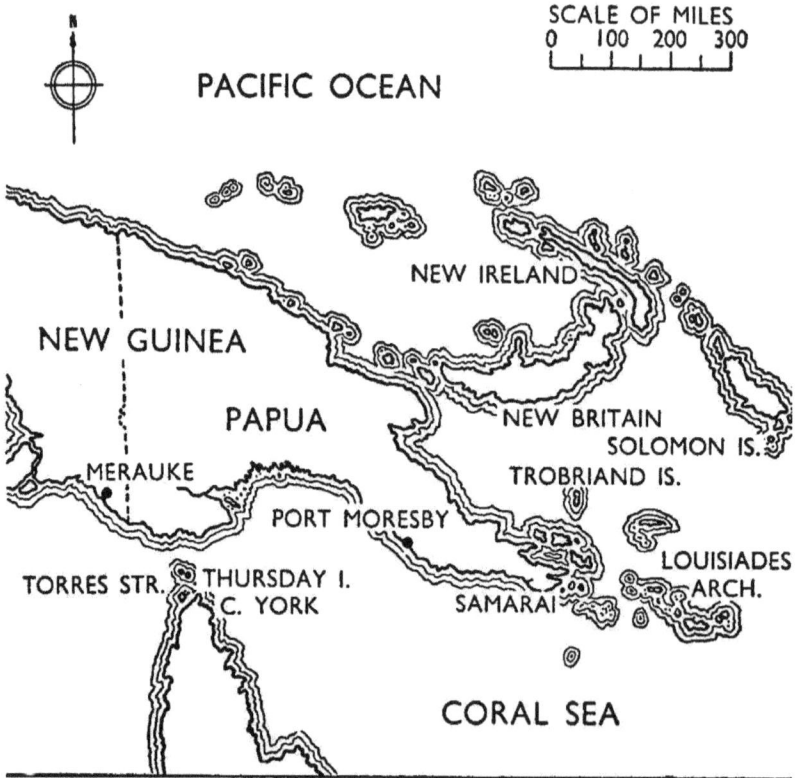

IN THIS story, the "suicide" of the plantation man in the fullness of his health and strength, and with apparently all the world before him, was only solved some years after the sorcerer's death, As a casual wanderer I was always interested in native life, and I have tried to put the native "whispers" together to trace the events that developed to the ultimate end.

In those days a chief sorcerer, working in the background, often held power of life and death over his tribesmen. Greatly dreaded, the acknowledged heads among them were very cunning, and occasionally could even destroy a white man. As happened in this case.

Tom, tom, tom, tom - though Ralston sneered at the drum's challenge he was worried indeed. Morosely, he leant upon the bungalow veranda. A dead end met his eye. The stacks of unhusked nuts, thousands of them. Those other brown stacks ready husked, just lying there. Valuable copra waiting in the drying sheds - waiting! The bags of finished stuff, and other bags half filled, which would presently begin to smell. A big job abandoned, as if a plague had banished the workers. *Tom, tom* - £2000 - apparently now doomed to ruin. *Tom, tom, tom, tom* - all because of these cursed nigger superstitions.

Before him spread to the water's edge gentle slopes crowned with palms now luxuriantly repaying twenty years' hard toil and care - his life - work. Blue water glimmered across the strait speckled with wooded islets, and in the distance rose the gloomy crags of Erromangan hills. A billowy haze was fleecy clouds veiling distant New Guinea. Overshadowing the foreshore, the baby mountains of his home island, jungle-clad upon moss-green rocks black at heart as this island's history. His bungalow was a picture, modern, too, even to a flowered lawn.

Tom, tom, tom, tom - curse that drum! Driving him mad, ceaselessly beating for three racking days and nights - the monotony of it, each distinct beat never varying in time and tone - *tom, tom* -

Ralston abruptly levelled his glasses out to sea, though he knew it was useless. The schooner was not due until next month to load the copra. Would that copra be ready?

"Blast Gambobo!" *Tom, tom* - he glared towards the big village sun-bathed among the mangoes. Its orderly grass houses showed abundant life-idle life. The women were away in the manioc gardens, but numerous brown youngsters laughed and howled and squabbled under the house supports, shooting reed arrows at one another and at grunting porkers, or varying their fun by torturing a screeching cockatoo that had barely three feathers left to its nakedness. Hefty men squatted on the platforms, gossiping, smoking, loafing - sneering towards him, hundreds of eyes covertly watching him. Defiantly his gaze rested on the Sacred House, the gigantic structure with its towering sides of palm matting so finely plaited that no woman could peep in, even should she dare. Its entrance platform on tall piles, the trunks of massive trees, was built to represent the open jaws of crocodiles. Under the thatched veranda which was the "roof" of the mouth, squatted the seniors of the cult.

Niggers! Planning the downfall of a white man's labours of twenty years and more!

Bitterly Ralston now regretted sneering at the Howling God. He had sailed here, just one lone white man into a savage stronghold, and carved out a fine plantation, careful always to give the natives no offence, always apparently sympathizing with, and never murmuring against, their customs and beliefs. Disaster had struck in one unguarded moment-after twenty years! Worry did it, short temper and exasperation and the anxiety to turn his fine crop of nuts into copra on a rising market. In the middle of work the villagers had calmly asked for a week off, for presently the nor'-west season would usher in the propitiation ceremonies to the Howling God. Ralston had refused, had sneered that the howl of the cyclone was merely the force of the wind, and not the voice of a god who would vindictively uproot villages if he were not propitiated. Next day not a soul had returned to work. To his commands, offers of rewards, entreaties, threats, they maintained a sullen silence. Their attitude was passive.

Never before, he felt, had he realized the full meaning of "passive."

Tom, tom, tom, tom - Ralston wished the Sacred House would collapse and crush that accursed drum. Its every beat signified a curse upon him, tolling a native requiem; he prayed that they would get on with the curse and silence the drum. He could fight the curse - if they would only start work!

What a peevish fool he had been. All this through one slip in twenty years! Of course, Gambobo was at the bottom of it, the sorcerer had everything to lose, his power over eight hundred people would be gone should they once lose fear of their native gods. Every island sorcerer hates the white man. His coming has dwindled their power to that of mere bogey-men.

Tom, tom, tom - Ralston stiffened, an angry frown on his lean brown face as Gambobo appeared from among the palms, came limping confidently across the garden.

They exchanged glare for glare. Gambobo meant everything his eyes said. Bloodshot eyes and cruel, they were devilishly shrewd. His skin was scarred by the storms of age, his upper lip missing for a dying victim had chewed it off. His lean neck was encircled by the human knuckle-bones of his calling; his withered body wore nothing else, which again was ominous. *Tom, tom, tom, tom* -

"You hear the drum, white man! It beats that you must die." Gambobo grinned hideously.

"Get to hell out of this," blazed Ralston, "before I flatten your carcass with a bullet."

"You would never dare!" The sorcerer leered. "For then the white-man police would come and make you trouble."

"Yes," answered Ralston instantly, "and if you interfere with me the white police will come and string you up by the neck."

"Not if you die by your own hand," said Gambobo meaningly, "for *that* we cannot help."

Ralston stared, astounded. Tom, tom -

"Don't you understand, white man?" insinuated the sorcerer in a wheedling voice. "We will kill you, but you will be slain by the Drum, which will destroy you by your own hand. And for that we cannot be held to blame."

Ralston gazed speechless. Tom, tom, tom, tom, tom, tom -

"I never took you for a fool before," said Ralston heavily, "but now I know you are an idiot! How on earth are you going to make me kill myself?"

Gambobo's lipless grin was dreadful. He cocked his. head to one side, a withered hand held in the attitude of listening. *Tom, tom, tom, tom, tom, tom -*

"Go," snarled Ralston, "or I'll boot you lively! And listen one moment! If the whole village is not at work tomorrow morning I'll spend the rest of my life proving to them what an impostor you are. I'll make you an outcast, I'll teach them to scorn you like a village mongrel. Go!"

Gambobo went, grinning evilly. Ralston strode indoors, his brain in turmoil. He was shivering a bit, too. He would take ten grains, just in case. Heavens, it would be awful now if he developed malaria and raved to the beat of that wretched drum!

The medicine chest was bare of quinine. He stared aghast, then searched frenziedly. Then sat down to think. *Tom, tom, tom, tom, tom, tom -*

He walked the room. He could not understand how he had run out of the most essential medicine of the tropics - he who was always so careful of a plentiful supply. And no chance of getting any for a month. Heavens! He *was* developing fever. No, it was only imagination. What an idiot he was, shivering at a very thought, just because he knew now he had no remedy! He pulled himself together. Curse that drum! It was even vibrating the house. He unhooked a brass tray from the wall, breathing relievedly as it ceased its gentle tremor.

Determinedly he walked out to the drying sheds and commenced husking nuts, jamming each down on the spiked bar with quick and practised hand. As he tore off each strip of husk the harsh sound was pleasant. Drive him mad, would they, the fools! *Tom, tom, tom, tom* - this was a relief, anyway. He could never strip all those thousands of nuts alone in time, of course, but this would keep his mind occupied. *Tom, tom -*

He slaved until late evening, then had his supper within closed doors. The beat of the drum was barely muffled. He lay awake feverishly tossing until the small hours. *Tom, tom, tom, tom -*

For three more days Ralston husked, snatching a nut from the heap, grasping it between his two palms as he brought it nearly forehead high to slam it down side on upon the sharp-pointed iron stake - *tom* - to lever the nut sideways so that the husk was wrenched and torn - *tom* - to grasp that strip with clawing fist - *tom* - and tear it from unwilling nut - *tom* - then up with the nut again and down - *tom* - to wrench the torn husk again - three, four times - *tom* - then throw aside the husked nut and grab another - *tom* -

Even on the afternoon of the first day he found himself trying to beat the rhythm. Angrily he tried to thrust the thought away, but each distinct action, each blow, each wrench he made in husking nut after nut he was trying to upset that *tom, tom, tom, tom* -

By afternoon of the third day he was rhythmically husking nuts to the drum-beat - *tom, tom, tom, tom* -

On the fourth day he strode determinedly down the bungalow steps, striding past the sheds with their heaps of nuts and half-dried copra without a glance. He would try a good, long walk to break the monotony of that rhythmical beat. He strode, unconsciously walking faster - *tom, tom, tom, tom* - right out through the plantation onto a well-trodden jungle track - *tom, tom, tom, tom,* monotonously following - *tom, tom* - he broke into a run to out-distance the sound, but pulled up short, rating himself soundly.

He strode on faster, wiping his hot brow. He did not know it, but he now looked as he felt, fearfully worried. *Tom, tom, tom, tom* - he became acutely aware the sound was not diminishing. He hurried on through forest track and jungle right into the depths of the hills - *tom, tom, tom, tom* - the drum now paced with his very steps - left, right, left, *tom,* left, *tom,* left, *tom,* left, *tom* - they - it - following him - wherever he went!

Ralston sat on the edge of the bed looking haggard indeed, feeling worse. His ears were plugged with cotton wool. If he could only sleep! He listened with strained face, then, as a child tempts a sore tooth, carefully pulled out the wool - *tom, tom, tom, tom* - hastily he replugged his ear. He started the gramophone to a fox-trot, but the thing looked inane, the disc spinning round soundlessly. He pulled the wool from his ears and grinned at the blare of jazz - *tom, tom, tom, tom* - in time to the dance. If the cursed drum would only miss a beat, anything to defeat for a moment its mathematical monotony. He tried again and again to start the gramophone so that it would not keep time with the drum. In a fit of maniacal rage, he threw it out of the window.

And now he could feel the drum vibrating through his brain as distinctly as if his ears were not plugged. In the early hours he jumped up and packed a few things. He would risk a trip to the mainland and bring over help of some kind. He could, he *would* sail the cutter alone.

He hurried down to the beach. The dinghy was afloat, gently drifting out with the tide. Strange! It had been securely anchored ashore. Hurriedly he stripped and plunged in, swimming with powerful strokes. The dinghy glided out just ahead of him. Ralston increased his stroke, then paused in growing surprise. The water was at full tide - there was no current -what then was making the dinghy drift? A cold uneasiness gripped him, and at that moment clawing hands swirled him completely under. He rose, gasping, and struck back in blind, unreasoning fear for the shore - *tom, tom, tom, tom* - he raced for the house, understanding that no matter how far he ran or how fast that drum-beat would keep time with him - for ever!

He locked himself in, shivering. From force of habit he opened the medicine chest as the terror of malaria faced him again - of course there was no quinine! Those dogs had stolen it long ago - *tom, tom, tom, tom* -

Sleep - he must have sleep. He rooted out a bottle of brandy. He was a non-drinker, but in trade etiquette it was essential to keep a case in the bungalow - *tom, tom, tom* -

His glaring eyes did not notice the trembling of his hands as he poured out a glassful. He would put himself to sleep, anyway - *tom, tom, tom, tom* - curse them! They could *tom-tom* for ever for all he cared! The spirit burnt his throat and he cursed it, too. He gulped enough to put four men to sleep, then locked the door, barred and shuttered the windows, and crawled under the mosquito net. His head buzzed with hundreds of drum-beats as he closed his eyes, smiling foolishly. Ah! He had put 'em out of time, if nothing else. His throbbing head subsided to a confused murmur as with a deep, tired sigh he fell asleep.

Hours later, feeling that he was struggling up from a deathly trance, he was fighting as if to attain consciousness in some life beyond. A ghostly light enshrouded him. Far away there seemed to beat a drum. Very dose breathed a something, a presence that raised his hair on end. There reached out towards him a frightful thing, a leprous hand with fingers pawing at his throat!

Ralston screamed, flung himself through the mosquito net, clawed the door in frantic terror - *tom, tom, tom, tom* - utter darkness - and a something waiting inside here with him. The sting of his broken fingernails brought realization that he was clawing at a locked door. A glimmering of reason returned, bringing cunning to fight against terror. He would not unlock it - no! He crouched back, listening - *tom, tom, tom, tom* - with his heart pounding thunderously. Nothing more, except a something. And it could not get out! Could it be Gambobo, the sorcerer who was drumming him mad? He would drum no more!

His heart beating more normally, he sneaked his way round the room, unaware of the glow in his glaring eyes. In a maniacal triumph he touched the bed and worked his hand up along it, then under the pillow feeling for the automatic and torch. With the flood of light he wheeled round, ready to fire instantly. There was not a thing in the room!

He peered under the bed, around the furniture. There was no one in the room but himself. His teeth chattering he fumbled at the medicine chest. Idiot! Gambobo had stolen the quinine ages ago!

Tom, tom, tom, tom - in a fury he dragged the bed aside.

How heavy the cursed thing had grown! He tore up the floor matting and examined the boards beneath. He was bitterly disappointed, for they were not sawn through, there was no man-hole. Automatically he wheeled the bed back, thinking, thinking. God! Surely it was never possible that the big-gun sorcerers could really materialize spirits of the evil dead and command them to obsess humans! He knew it was whispered, was implicitly believed by the natives.

He turned the lamp full up, sat on the edge of the bed, and buried his head in his hands, trying to press out the certainty that there was a something in the room - *tom, tom, tom, tom* -

From behind him, from under the tumbled blankets, as silent as any shadow, there slipped a shrivelled black form to vanish under the bed.

Tom, tom, tom, tom - Ralston sobbed aloud. He knew he would go mad if he did not soon get sleep. And now he was afraid to sleep. He lay back on the bed and gazed at the ceiling, deliberately listening - *tom, tom, tom, tom, tom* -

At daylight he crept out to the kitchen. He no longer heard the birds calling these mornings, because of the beating drum.

He triumphed before midday, though - drank a bottle of brandy and fell asleep. He was very cunning about it. They would not know by day, they would thump and thump and he would be asleep all the time while they thump - thumped - and he could watch by night!

They could not wake him until late afternoon. He dreamt he was tossing within a cloud of thunder, it reverberated so it almost burst his ear drums. In drunken re-awakening he strove to think-they must have brought the drum right into the house. In drunken fury he searched for the rifle then staggered out to the veranda - *tom, tom, tom, tom* - They were away among the palms now. He staggered down among the palms, following the sound, but presently realized the drum was in the Sacred House again - *tom, tom, tom, tom, tom, tom* - In mental torture he crawled homeward.

Darkness brought the terror that he might fall asleep and It might come again. He walked the veranda, automatically falling into step - left, *tom* left, *tom*, left, *tom*, left, *tom*, left -

His reason was twitching and he knew it-it would snap at this rate. Suddenly the brandy demons gave him a great idea. Laughingly he snatched the rifle and ran down the village path and straight along to their Sacred House. With frenzied strength he sprang up the notched ladder leading to the broad platform. He would settle the drum!

Squatting figures did not move as he staggered towards the doorway. He was inside a slanting laneway of coconut matting, then stepped into the barn like building. Quite dark and evil and musty smelling - and a cathedral-like silence - *tom, tom, tom, tom* - the drum seemed beckoning from outside now - he flashed on the torch. It illuminated a laneway of shadows, the roof loomed fifty feet above. He tiptoed down the aisle, matting covered. like sentinels along each side rose the trunks of trees supporting the roof. The torch flashed on a bunch of dried heads. Along both sides were dim cubicles, in each a squatting figure. Ralston felt they were going to spring out on him from behind, but never a man moved. Initiates, these shadow men, being instructed into the mysteries of the unseen, just before warriorhood. His torch blazed on sheaves of weapons and huge, bestial masks. Dim skulls were necklaced from cubicle to cubicle, they grinned knowingly, sneeringly at him - *tom, tom, tom, tom* - in despair he halted as if an invisible hand held him from penetrating towards the darker mysteries of the sorcerer's latticed quarters. He laughed derisively - in hollow derision the sound was swallowed by the building. The penalty was death for the unbidden to enter this House. He defied them aloud-they could not kill him twice! *Tom, tom* - he wheeled with the revolver outstretched, but nothing had moved.

The drum was not here - *tom, tom, tom, tom* - yes, awaiting him outside!

He staggered out and marked the sound as coming from the dense shadows of the mango-trees. Craftily he approached - and then the drum mocked from away across near the bungalow.

Despairingly he made for the sea beach, seeking the silent peace of the shore. Left, *tom*, left, *tom*, left, *tom*, left -

Dawn found him wearily climbing the veranda, to gaze in despair towards the Sacred House. *Tom, tom, tom, tom* - When the sun dissolved its shadowed gloom he dragged out a heavy case. Surprising how strong he still was! He spread a rug and opened out the cartridge boxes, smiling in malicious anticipation. The villagers, watching among the palms, quietly disappeared.

Ralston lay on the rug - *tom, tom, tom, tom* - the village was nicely within range. He blazed furiously at the Sacred House, scattering his shots all along the great walls. "Crack!" - *tom*- "Crack!" - *tom* - "Crack!" - *tom* -"Crack!"

- *tom* - swiftly he reloaded - "Crack!" - tom - "Crack!" - *tom* - with a litter of empty shells around him he laughed to the skies, then, ominously bright-eyed, peered forward to listen - *tom, tom, tom, tom* - wearily he pressed his temples, pathetically his head dropped to the boards. How muffled the drum was becoming, why, it was fainting! He jerked upright - *tom, tom, tom, tom* - from his very bedroom! He rushed inside, then out again as from the palms - *tom, tom, tom, tom* - he blazed at palm after palm until the barrel grew hot, he threw the rifle from him, and laughed through the bungalow - *tom, tom, tom, tom, tom, tom* -

That evening Ralston smiled very cunningly - it did not matter at all that now he could scarcely walk. The silly fools - why, it was necessary to crawl now to beat them! *Tom, tom, tom, tom* - he ground his teeth in silent mirth. Soon he would silence it - definitely - he hugged the matches in his hand.

He crawled to the banana patch and peered across the cleared ground that merged into the grotesque shadow of the Sacred House. *Tom, tom, tom, tom* - a bony hand touched his neck - he screamed.

"Don't do it, white man!" Gambobo leered down at him.

"Why not?" whispered Ralston .

The sorcerer knelt beside him, his eyes gleaming in the night.

"Because you would burn the secrets of the present Past!" he hissed. "Because - we would smear your naked body with honey and stretch you out on an ants' nest - you would die vainly - for when the white police came we would point to the burnt House and they would go away, for even no white man dare burn down our Sacred House! We wish you to die without harming us - for thus the Howling God has spoken. And when it has come about I, his priest, will have gained great prestige among all the people."

Ralston flicked up his automatic, but the sorcerer easily snatched it away.

"White man," he whispered persuasively, "to go forward means a living death with the ants. You desire sleep, above all things - it is yours. So easily, so quickly." He stared into Ralston's widening eyes. "Go back to your bed and - sleep!"

He tapped the automatic significantly, handed it to Ralston, and vanished. *Tom, tom, tom, tom, tom, tom* - Ralston clawed at a banana stem and staggered upright. Sleep! The thought overwhelmed him, overwhelmed everything. Why had he not thought of it before? Why, it would even overwhelm the drum - he could have sleep - *tom, tom* - he staggered back towards the bungalow - *tom, tom, tom, tom…*

15

THE TIN-MAKERS

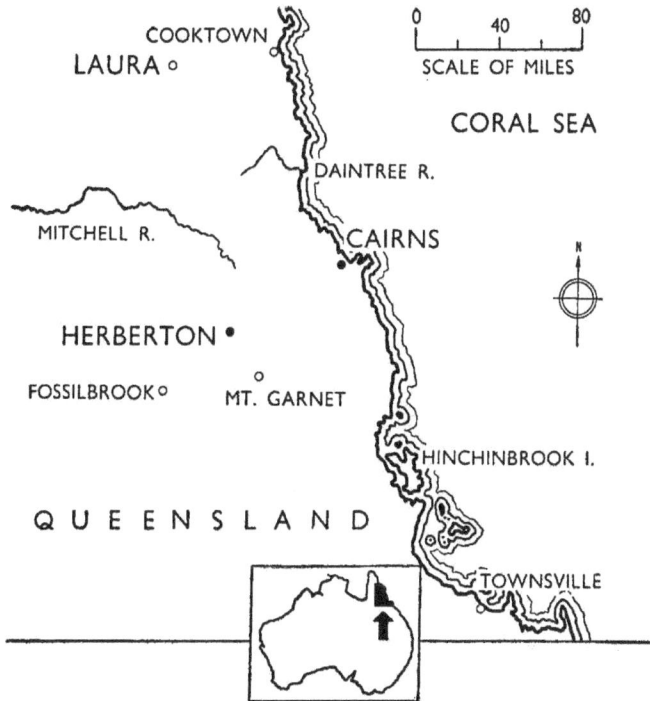

FOR THE better understanding of this story, please know that the prospector-miner lives on hope, and the will-o'-the-wisp of that particular mineral or gem that lures him on. Especially is this so in the dogged work and hopes of the gold-, opal-, sapphire-, and tin-miners. Each one lives and sleeps with the star he seeks. The gold-digger's work and mind is "Gold! Gold! Gold!" while many a time his tired body twitches with golden dreams of nights. So also with the opal-gouger. And the tin-scratcher. At their camp-fires at night naturally they talk "gold" or "opals" or "tin".

And often and often they discuss and wonder just how in the first place these elusive wealths of their dreams were formed. Yes, often and often - as I myself have done.

Sometimes a man's theory appears very close to fact, that is, to what in our limited knowledge we believe the fact to be. Yet again, a man's theory may be fantastic - especially in the case of those lone men who work, and think, and wonder, and brood alone.

The story here, though, is of no such theory. Unless, of course, the grizzled old tale-teller had really thought out his belief but hid his seriousness under the cloak of a tale. I have known men tell their true beliefs in such ways.

In this story I, a stranger coming into the district, had been warned, though with a kindly grin, that my mate was "the biggest liar unhung".

Maybe so. But he proved a good old mate to me.

"Thud! Thud!"

The pick strokes echoed dully in the tunnel where the two miners worked far in under the ridge of the Herberton Deep Lead. Far up through the solid rock roof the blue sky of North Queensland shone over range and river, over the hamlets of men, over horses and cattle and singing birds. But down here the gloomy, deathlike quietness was only broken by that "Thud! Thud! Thud!"

The grizzled old miner squatting upon his haunches dropped his pick with a grunt and, reaching towards the tobacco tin, growled amiably "Smoke-ho!" to his mate who was kneeling at the face they were toiling at, peering at the dull, water-worn stones and gravels by the feeble light of a candle. His most searching examination showed only scantily, here and there among the pebbly wash-dirt, little, such very little, seams of what looked like jet-black sand - in reality, precious grains of the black stream tin they were toiling so hard for with such woeful return. Yes, just a feeble, a broken, wishy-washy seam of stream tin. A poor-looking prospect indeed.

The greybeard, empty pipe gripped between leathery lips, slowly, efficiently rubbing tobacco between the palms of gnarled old hands, quizzically watched the serious face of his young mate, illuminated by the dull yellow flame, as it peered anxiously for signs of payable quantities of the little black grains that would settle the store-keeper's bill.

With stubby thumb ramming the tobacco "just right" down into that charcoal-encrusted pipe-bowl, the grey-beard grinned quietly down in under his whiskers. He had humped matilda many and many a mile with empty tucker-bags, had crossed many a dry gully in his time. His young mate had all his heartbreaks before him. Reaching out, he calmly took the candle from the young fellow's hand, lit his smelly pipe with three slow puffs, hooked the candle spider to a timber, and leant contentedly back against the tunnel wall.

"Strange!" He puffed thoughtfully. "This bouldery wash-dirt was once a big old-man river-bed. Queer fishes swum in it an' gobbled one another up with might and main. Chased hell outer one another an' made love an' did all sorter things. And animals bigger 'n' elephants played an' fought an' howled an' yelled along its banks."

"Um!" replied his mate as he wedged a prop in place beneath the dangerous roof and jammed, then hammered the wooden cap well home.

"Yes," went on the greybeard, "an' them scientist blokes reckon we was oncest them fishes what grew legs an' lorst our tails an' eventually grew to what we are now - two blanky tin-scratchers scratching away for tin in the very river-bed we once lived and swum in."

"Um!" grunted his mate as with a sigh he sat back against the wall. "I wish your petrified old river would make a few bags of tin for us - how wonderful it would be if we could only strike a real patch! If we don't strike a few bags soon it will mean the swag for me! Pass me the tobacco - thanks! Anyway, how do you account for our finny ancestors living through all the molten lava that flowed into this old river and filled it up? Reckon that kills your precious theory as it killed the fishes. I wonder under what conditions this tin was first formed, all the same."

The greybeard gazed benignly at his sun-tanned young mate. The old digger dearly loved a yarn, and this innocent-looking boy would at least hear him out, even if he did believe him a liar afterwards.

"Well," he said slowly, between puffs, "I will tell you a yarn that proves we have lived through the lava, and answer your question at the same time. And as this ridge top is hangin' above us, it's the living truth.

"You've heard 'em talking back there in Herberton town," he declared solemnly, "you've heard 'em talking of the Black Swan, the claim I got my big rise out of?"

I nodded. For I was the young fellow in this story. "Well, one mornin' before I found that luverly show I strolls to work feeling pretty moody like, bein' up to my eyeballs in debt, an' Jack and Newell not too happy about it - the good God only knows how many 'hard lucks' they had on their books at that time. Anyway, I crawls into me tunnel knowin' there was not one pin-head of tin showin' in the face. It was the rainy season, the water was beginning to seep through the tunnel roof; in the night it had collected in a fair-sized, clear little pool where I'd worked the day before, damn' chilly it looked in the candlelight. I stood there wonderin' if it was worth while to drain the water out, or whether it wouldn't be better to chuck up the show and try somewheres else. Movin' the candle about, I notice some wee bubbles rising slowly up through the water, right against the wash-dirt. I held down the candle and bent over, looking more closely, and there, clinging to the wash-dirt was a cluster of wee brown eggs, each about the size of a grain of tin.

"At first I thought it really was tin, but while I looked each grain separated from the bunch, sent up a few quivery little bubbles, then before my very eyes each egg hatched out a tiny insect. I knew I wasn't drunk, hadn't had the price of a drink even, for the larst twelve months! I rubbed my eyes and looked close, feeling startled like you know, down there in that darkness an' quietness, all alone with only a tiny candle-flame an' me mind all worried like. But I wasn't seein' things, them eggs had all gone and there was dozens of swimming insects, jumping and whirling about like tiny fireworks torpedoes.

"You see, they must have been eggs laid millions and millions of years ago, before all that molten lava flowed into the river and made it a river no more. The spark of life was still smouldering in them eggs, and now that prehistoric conditions of life they were used to living under had come back to them, that is, the water, they just simply hatched. Wonderful thing this Nature!"

"Yes." I grinned. "I've read of scientists finding grain and seeds in old Egyptian tombs, and forcing them to life by artificial means. Go on."

"Yes, that's it exactly," agreed the greybeard enthusiastically. "I sees as you're a bit learned yourself, young Feller-me-lad. Well, these there insects grew until they were about the size of a match-head, and in shape like tiny crayfish, all arms and whirling legs. And me kneelin' down there on me knees with the candle watchin' them, that interested I didn't notice the water creeping half-way to me knees. After a good while I discovers they were working together like mad, but with some queer system. An employin' capitalist would have gone crazy if he could have been there and calculated the amount of work they was toiling at for their size, compared with that of a man.

"It took about an hour before I drops to what they were at-an' when I seen through it I near fell dead!" The grey-beard took the pipe from his mouth, slowly refilled, lit up, his eyes full of wonderment gazing at me all the time. So silent was the gloomy tunnel that I could hear us breathing.

With a deep, deep breath, he resumed. "About fifty of 'em was diggin' out little grains of red sand from the wash-dirt, and swimmin' with it to the fellers at the face. These catches the sand an' pounds an' pulls it, their little legs flyin' like the arms of a windmill, sendin' up tiny bubbles to the top of the water. When the manufacturin' process was over, three of 'em catches hold of the result, which was a single grain of black sand, and swims with it to the face, where they jammed it into a growing, black seam. They was makin' tin! Makin' stream tin!"

He paused dramatically, and I felt his bright eyes beneath those shaggy brows upon me. But I gazed thoughtfully down at the water-worn boulders in the old riverbed.

"As soon as I understood what they were at," the gruff old voice continued, "I nearly spoils the whole thing with excitement. I stands up sudden an' laughs an' shouts, knocking a little heap of mullock with a splash into the water. I near panicked, 'cause if I'd killed any of those insects I believe I should have cried.

"I'd begun to see what a good thing I had on. Running out of the tunnel to the creek, I fetches up two buckets of water and empties 'em into the pool, because I wanted the little toilers to have as much play as possible, an' besides, there might be more eggs lyin' about waitin' to be hatched.

"By dinner-time I'd carried so much water I had to block the tunnel mouth up a foot to hold the water back; I forgot all about the water drippin' through the roof all the time. Just before knock-off time I had another good look at the insects.

"Sure as life they'd built up a seam of stream tin half an inch thick, and two foot long. They was workin' exactly like coral insects, only instead of useless limestone they was buildin' up good stream tin. I felt so happy I sat there in the water an' laughed, tryin' to pick out the gangers and wonderin' which gang of 'em was toilin' the hardest.

"I tried to count 'em, but they was swimmin' backwards and forwards so fast it wasn't possible. I got to two hundred and sixty-five three times when I noticed the little fellers who did the carrying was in difficulties. They was making desperate efforts to reach with their little feelers a band of bright red sand that ran about half an inch above the surface of the water, a bright red, oxide of iron sort of sand. The toilers were swimming about the face like mad, angry at having nothing to do.

"The Brain works an' I got the pick an' knocks some of the red sand into the water, careful not to hurt a single insect. And sure enough they dives straight to the bottom after that red sand and starts carryin' it to the experts at the face. They bucks in to make up for lost time, poundin' the sand into grains of tin an' jammin' 'em in the face.

"I nearly went crazy when I knew I'd dropped to the secret. I had the insects that made the tin, an' I'd found out the stuff to feed 'em with!

"You can bet I gouged out a few barrow-loads of that red sand quick an' lively and put it in the water close to the carters, so as they wouldn't have to swim far to reach it, and so lose time.

"That night I hardly slept a wink. I could see a for¬tune before me, an' every time I thought of the insects I nearly went silly with laughin' for pure joy, an' then gettin' deadly afraid someone'd find it out and steal 'em away. Twice I got up an' walked through the scrub to the tunnel, to make sure no one was about.

"I lay awake for hours calculating and planning how long it would take those two hundred and sixty-five insects to build up a bag of tin. Every time the calculations worked out at a bag a week. That meant over six quid, and at first I was quite satisfied, believe me.

"But as I lay there I kept wonderin' if I couldn't make 'em work harder, or make the carriers carry twice as much red sand. If they was only makin' a bag of tin a day now, instead of one a week! Then I grew scared if I worked 'em overtime they might play up, might even go on strike, which would be real cruel. Then I gets wonderin' couldn't I now make tin meself? That red sand seemed a sort of cement. But then they knows how to work it up an' I don't. Come to think of it, the coral insect can make limestone, my insects could make tinstone, I could make neither. The more you comes to think on it, the more wonderful Nature is. Come to think on it, Nature even made me!"

The greybeard sighed deeply, thoughtfully refilled his pipe, the silence emphasized by our breathing, and a soft "Drip! Drip! Drip!" from the roof.

"Howsomenever," he resumed mournfully, "I hurries to work with the dawn next mornin' an' gets two pleasant surprises. First, I sees by the amount of tin they'd made that they'd toiled right through the night. I'd calculated on 'em workin' three shifts, eight hours a time, like you an' me, knockin' orf for a spell an' a feed an' a sleep. So you can guess how pleased I was with me willing little workers. But what made me gasp with joy was a cluster of neat brown eggs glued on the side of a quartz boulder sticking in the wash-dirt.

"I fair danced with joy when I saw them eggs. You see, them little toilers was not only working for me dayan' night; they was attendin' to family affairs also. And now my calculations of the night before went up with a bound - they was makin' ever so much more tin than I thought they could, an' there was goin' to be so many more of 'em! God bless 'em!

"The heap of red sand I'd knocked out for 'em the night before was nearly all used up, so I got a sweat up gouging out a few barrow-loads more so as not to keep 'em waiting for building material. Then I tried to count the eggs, but they was too small.

"However, I guessed there must be an egg a man, or else the lady insects had laid two eggs apiece, an' then gone straight on with their good work.

"I felt so satisfied with my little gang I pulls out my pipe to have a smoke while waiting for these new eggs to hatch. And sure enough, just before crib time out came the little things, kickin' an' swimmin' just as their parents did before them.

"I gouged out more red sand, because now the numbers was doubled they'd need double the quantity of tin-buildin' material. However, they didn't grow big enough for work until about four o'clock, when they bucked in at the face same as their parents did afore 'em.

"That night I lay awake and calculated again, though I was so excited me brain could see nothing but a mountain of tin, with great long-legged animals pounding up red sand and shovellin' it on the mountain where it rolled down the sides pure stream tin.

"However, I calculates at last that the first lot made about fifteen pounds weight of tin for an eight hours' shift, then each mornin' there was a fresh gang on, an' the mornin' after that there'd be two more gangs, an' so on. And as the first gang worked the whole twenty-four hours I calculated a result for the week that made my head dizzy.

"I daren't calculate beyond a week, my poor excited brain just couldn't stand it.

"Well, each mornin' there was a fresh batch of eggs, an' soon I had all my time cut out feedin' the red sand to the insects, now increasin' like a gathering army. You know a good deal of the rest. The Black Swan proved to be the best tin-producer Herberton ever seen, an' I could have sold her again an' again.

"I was very careful, of course, wouldn't let anyone into the tunnel, pitching my camp a few yards away so that I could hear if any inquisitive busy-bodies came nosing about during the night.

"Well, things got that way at last I was nearly killed with overwork. I seemed to be doing nothing but feedin' the insects with red sand and takin' the tin away from them. And calculatin' - always calculatin'. I got poor as a horse-rake, what with excitement and no sleep, and I was afraid I was goin' to be laid up with brain fever.

"That first week I bagged half a ton of tin, but before the next week the tin increased so much I had to pay men to bag it outside the tunnel, as it took me all my time truckin' it away from the insects. In a couple of months I'd sold over five thousand pounds' worth of tin that my little army of tin manufacturers had made.

"But the quicker the money rolled in the more I wanted it to roll more. I used to lay awake wonderin' an' wonderin' if I could put somethin' in the water to make 'em work faster, or if only I could coax 'em to lay two eggs instead of one. I even got thinkin' of twins. My head got so dazed at last with thinking and overwork that I could hardly stand. I worked hard trying to figure out that one about encouragin' 'em to have twins, but got scared lest I interfere in their family affairs. Insects is a bit touchy that way you know, same as we are. But I thought such a lot about it I blame the thinking part for what happened.

"For three nights I couldn't sleep a wink, and on the fourth I walks a couple of miles to the Nigger Creek pub and buys me a bottle or two of rum. A few nips would make me sleep better, I thought. Just as an appetizer, I has a few at the pub.

"When I got back to the camp I swilled a good strong nip, then two more as chasers. Which after a coupla others makes me feel a lot better and steadies me head, but just as I was tum in' into bunk the devil whispers, 'Why not go an' drink good luck to them poor little insects workin' all night in the cold water makin' tin for you?' Like a damn' fool I opens another bottle an' gets a light and walks into the tunnel.

"The insects was workin' away like mad, hundreds an' hundreds of 'em, workin' so hard it made the surface of the water look like a fairy fountain with the little bubbles they was kickin' up.

"I was so overjoyed at their goodness to me that I leans against the wall of the tunnel and nearly cries for pure joy. I poured out half a pannikin of rum and, holding it above my head, I made a speech of thanks to them there insects.

"But they just went on workin'. The rum must have got into my head then, me being unsteady in the brain, because I drank the whole lot neat until that bottle was empty, too.

"Me head was turnin' round and round an' I flops into the water in the tunnel, thinkin' I was climbing into me bunk.

"The splash put the candle out and wakes me up a bit, cause I starts off shiverin' towards the tunnel mouth, gropin' at the walls with tremblin' hands.

"All I remember is cursin' an' prayin' an' seein' things like a man in the horrors when suddenly I staggered up against the boarding fixed in the mouth of the tunnel to dam the water back. I caught hold of it to steady myself when the whole thing collapsed, sending me sprawling with the water rushing out over me.

"It cleared my brain clear as it is now an' the dreadful horror I felt at what I'd done still wakes me up screamin' with nightmares.

"As the water was rushing away it was taking the insects with it, an' soon there wouldn't be a single insect left in the tunnel!

"I lay flat an' screamed and shouted for help, tryin' to keep the water back with my body, an' just mana gin' to save a little.

"All the camps around were woke by my yells, and in a couple of minutes half a dozen men were tearing through the scrub towards the tunnel. Sam Rolley an' Harry Bennet reached me first, and as soon as Sam sees me he says, 'Why, it's old Joe lyin' there in the water! He's got the horrors again.'

"They laid hold of me an' tries to pull me up, but I clawed to the ground and yelled to them to let me alone, to block up the tunnel an' save the insects!

"'He's got 'em bad this time,' says Sam. 'Get a half Nelson on the old blighter an' we'll carry him off to his bunk.'

"Harry grabs me legs and Sam me arms, and together they manhandles me away while in cryin' despair I saw the last few buckets of water flow away out the tunnel.

"When I saw what they'd done I let 'em do what they liked, which was to take me into Herberton hospital, where I was laid up for three months with brain fever. Not *rum* fever, as they all says I was.

"I was very nearly done for, I can tell you. When I came out they told me I was all the time howlin' out to block me insects.

"I sold the Black Swan afterwards to a company, who rushed at the chance of buying. I said as how I felt too broke up to work any more.

"Needless to say, the Black Swan produced no more tin. They worked it for twelve months and never got a bag."

16

HOW PETER FOUND HIS MOUNTAIN OF TIN

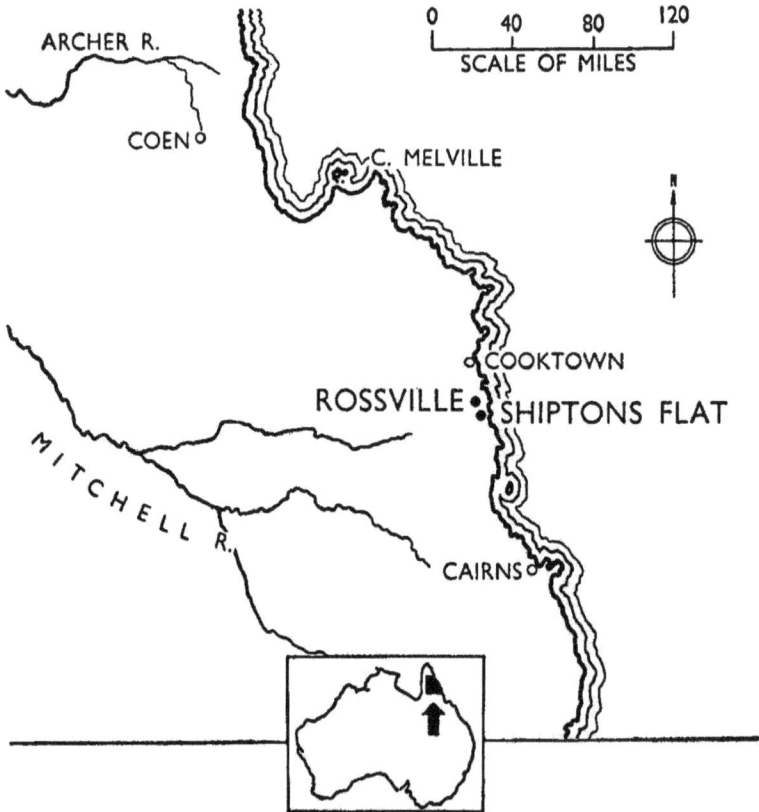

YET another story of the "power of the mind" working in the solitary lives of the gold- and tin-seekers of our Far North. Ever seeking fortune, ever thinking of it, ever wondering where it could be, thinking of it by day even while toiling, dreaming of it in their lonely camps by night.

No wonder that the urge of this ceaseless quest grows into their very bones. The milky quartz, the blue-grey slate, the yellow gold. That dark-grey basalt, the grey granite, the black stream tin. The glory of the hidden sapphire in the depths of some vanished stream, the desert sandstone of some vanished sea powerless to quench the blaze of the fiery opal!

Seek, and ye shall find!

Ah, and how we used to seek! Many of us, with our lives.

"We're crazy!" declared gruff old Peter Sloane. "We'll still be seeking when they wrap us in our blanket and 'bury us deep down below'. Our bones will go back to the clay and the granite even if they don't bottom us on gold." Which growling sentiments (eventually to come true in his case) led to his telling me this yarn, one sunset on the veranda of his hut as we lazed the evening away smoking while gazing up into the huge blackness that was Mount Finlayson. The wind was sighing away down in the cold, dank gorge, while high up, resting just upon the old mountain crown, a diadem of gold-dust which was stars twinkled in their everlasting mystery.

Fitting setting for a story such as this, with Peter the lonely little human sighing his life away for the hidden fortune that never would come his way.

Of course, I enjoyed and laughed at his story-with a sigh. For that story had already happened to me. And would again.

But here is old Peter's story. Our story-the story of all of us scattered among those mountains seeking fortune while living on the smell of an oiled rag and-hope!

Dog-tired and a bit downhearted, old Peter Sloane sat on his humpy veranda gazing wistfully at the huge bulk of Mount Finlayson, its granite ramparts just now capped by a cloud of mist.

A wandering geologist had told him that up there some-where was where the tin had come from, washed down by the rains of countless centuries onto the low-lying hills and flats, until at last in this present age man had come along with his pick and shovel in quest of the precious metal. The learned bloke had explained what a father of mountains this old mount must have been away back in those vanished centuries, with its great bulk then capped by enormous reefs of pure tin as yet untouched by the rains of ages, let alone man. Peter thought dolefully of his own poor claim, just a tucker claim. And now, this evening, all alone, he was thinking of the funny things that "eddicated" bloke had told him.

Darkness cloaked the grim mountain, there came the cold breath of night, but Peter still sat on as if trying to gaze into the very heart of the mountain in search of the mother lode that must be hidden there - still must be hidden there.

They watched it slowly sink, then gaped up again at Jemmy the Hook, leaning over the rail, grinning down at them.

With a start, Peter awoke-in a brilliant sunlight that fairly streamed through his whiskers. He was standing on an open forest hill, gazing dumbfoundedly at a mountain the like of which he had never seen before, except long ago in some hazy dream. To the very heavens its towering mass arose, its flanks stretching far away into distance. A menacing shadow pecked his feet and Peter leapt backward to run screaming like a terrified child for a sheltering clump of granite rocks. Darting into a fissure, he squirmed his body down into the farthest crack as the head of the gigantic eagle, screeching its baffled rage, pecked vainly down at him.

For hours Peter crouched terrified within the rock until, the agony of his cramped body becoming unbearable, he crawled to the fissure mouth and thrust his scared face out into the glorious sunlight. The eagle had vanished on more profitable business. At which Peter, gazing at the impenetrable scrub which clothed the foot of the mountain, felt hope surge within his numbed body. If only he could reach those sheltering trees this terrible bird could not possibly catch him. Not giving himself time to think, he darted into the open and raced for the scrub like any hard-pressed hare for its sanctuary. When just within yards of safety came a thud like a ton of bricks behind him! One fearful glance showed him the mother and father of all kangaroos ever born then or since. Like the hawse-hole of a liner was its pouch, from which protruded the head of a baby joey big as the head of an overgrown draught-horse.

One bound, and Peter was in the gloomy scrub tearing past its gnarled trees with the speed of a hunted soul. In the very heart of the scrub he stopped, panting, crouching low down in the Ranges of a friendly fig-tree.

As his wind came back, a vague indignation seized him:

Where the hell was he, anyway? What was the meaning of all this? What was the business of these giant fantods that chased a man as if he were only a damned rabbit?

He must make his way away down to Shipton's Flat and tell the blokes there what he'd seen at the foot of Finlayson. They'd come out with their guns then and these damned things would get hell and buckshot.

With a little more confidence, Peter stepped out through the scrub. He could not remember this overgrown scrub at all, everything was of the giant type that sneered down upon him as if he were a worm - he, Peter Sloane, nourishing a whisker like Abraham, six foot one in his socks - when he had any. Yes, six foot odd, and all bone from the neck up! A wild bee nearly blew his ear off as it roared past with all motors buzzing like an aeroplane. He shuddered back from a tree-trunk as a black-and-red striped tiger snarled out at him-by the time he'd caught his breath he saw it was only a meat-ant, a gigantic, aggressive ant the size and cheek of a butcher's pup, threatening Peter with a claw that could have ripped his wrist off. And what were these terrific things that seemed to be trees? Why, the butts of them were the size of a house. What a fortune for a timber man! But then, the saw was never made that could saw through trunks like these!

A stupid-looking grub, plainly a victim of overeating, gawked down at him from eyes big as a cow's, then over-balanced from its leaf and fell on his foot, nearly breaking it. To Peter's anguished howl an inquisitive lizard poked out its head - but Peter had vanished! One glance at that crocodile-like snout and he was racing for his life.

From the mountain now came a continuous, deafening roar. "What a whopper waterfall!" thought Peter. "That's not Hogan's Falls. I've never heard a Niagara like this before. Where in the name of Kingdom Come and Good King Saul am I? And as sober as a judge! Where in the name of this mysterious hell can I possibly be? And what brought me here? And how?"

Suddenly he stopped, abso-bally-lutely completely and definitely mystified now. For before him roared a torrential river fairly howling its head off in an overpowering urge to hurry somewhere, its bed strewn with overgrown boulders among which the rushing water raged and tore with a violence that completely overawed the pygmy man. But what was all this black sand that lay three feet deep at the river's edge? With heart beating a bit more humanly Peter walked towards the black sand, then with a delighted cry dropped on his knees among the stuff. It was pure stream tin.

Tons and tons and tons of it - thousands and thousands of tons of it! With the glad cry of a wandering human soul come home to roost, Peter buried his arms down up to the elbows in the precious black stuff and chucked it all up over himself and buried his arms down into it again as if he were swimming in a depthless sea of ten-pound notes. Ho! Ho! And so Peter Sloane owed the storekeeper twelve months' tucker money, did he? Well, now and here he'd found a river of tin that could buy up all the storekeepers in the world! And what did his not so trusting friend Bill the storekeeper with his dismal look have to say about it now? Those geologist blokes were right, though, give credit where credit is due. They'd assured him the tin is all coming from the big mountain. As the mountain was being washed away the tin was being swept down onto the Bat country, right away down onto Shipton's Flat. He'd never thought much of these school-learnin' geologists, but they were right this time! By gum, they were!

In a heaven of delight Peter Sloane glanced up as the laugh on his face froze to a horror that nearly choked him. There on the opposite bank, gawking across at h*im*, was a black gin - standing eight feet six inches in her bare pelt if she stood an inch! And she had plenty to stand with, believe me. Gripping a half-gnawed thigh-bone in one hand she was glaring across the river in a horrified sort of way, her broad body daubed with splashes of yellow ochre, her hair glued in a knob large as a show pumpkin with the help of a chunk of reddish clay. As Peter glared back the bone clattered from her hand, she lurched forward and with a resounding thud sprawled on the ground, the first and last aboriginal lady to faint. The sight of the white debil-debil had been too much for her.

It was not a sense of modesty that urged Peter slink back and By into the sheltering scrub as if the fiends of hell were at his heels. If that Lady with the Bone caught up with him he'd think all his birthdays had come at once! My Heavens, what an awful death! And he used to think a lot about women, too. This one would make him do more than think.

Exhausted and almost crying with fear he sank down by a broad creek and bent his fevered brow to the cool water. Instantly a shark-like creature snapped up at him with a clash of teeth like tempered steel, gushing a beastly breath full in his face. The terrified man, as he bounded high in the air and ran, knew he had met the father of all eels. Everything seemed to be a father of things in this damned place.

He must climb to the top of the mountain. There was nothing else for it. From there he could see his direction for home and Cooktown, that dear little township far away beside the sea. To get right away out of this accursed mystery land very quickly if not sooner was now Peter's one and urgent ambition.

For hours the wretched man climbed and panted and climbed with bleeding feet and torn hands, his body lacerated by the tearing thorns and clinging vines. At last, utterly exhausted and throwing up the sponge he sank down by a huge black boulder and, laying his poor face against the cool stone, began crying like a beaten child.

Something made him look at the stone, and look again.

He rose unbelievingly to his feet, then with a tremulous cry tried to clasp the great rock in both arms. It was tin, pure tin-it must weigh nearly forty tons! High in the air, he could see adhering to it a ragged edge of quartz. It was a specimen, washed down from some great reef higher up the mountain. All fatigue dropped from Peter. He ran round the boulder, and began climbing higher and higher. Huge junks of tin lay scattered on the mountain side. He must be very near the reef-the Father of all Tin Reefs-wealth untold. No one *would - could* believe it! What would the blokes in Rossville say? And those he-men tin-scratchers toiling at the Lion's Den.

What a rush there would be!

Then, right in front of him, stretched the reef. He could not see its cap, it reared high up among the tree branches.

And both its sides stretched farther away than he could see. In sheer awe he gazed at the black, dull mass.

This was the reef that had shed all the tin down onto the forest spurs and alluvial flats. The greatest reef in all the world!

Intense excitement gripped Peter Sloane. He turned and simply flew down the mountain. He *must* race to Cooktown and report this mighty find. He *must* bring out Warden Power. What a tremendous field this would be. Peter Sloane would be the most famous explorer in all Australia!

Jumping from rock to rock, tripping, falling, rising, his neck seemingly made of india-rubber, Peter plunged through the scrub at the mountain's foot. A great mottled cable vine was in his way, suspended between two tree-trunks. He reached out his arm to push it away and instantly was lifted high into the air. His career was at an end. The coils of the python were cracking his ribs, the saliva from its awful mouth sliming all over his body to oil it up for the swallow. It licked its chops.

As with a serpent-like hiss it opened wide a cavernous mouth and fastened down on him his lungs burst-crash.

For quite a time Peter lay there, scared stiff. And no wonder. In inky darkness, in awful terror feeling himself breathing deep down in here in the belly of the snake. Then he felt a surge of warm, comradely sympathy, for he heard the cat down in here with him. But then-a more plaintive "Meow!" sat him up in a disbelieving, delirious hope, his ears wide open now, then his mouth. Softly at first, in a tremulous delight he whispered some swear-words, then with a rapidly warming enthusiasm and fluency he recited all the naughty words he ever remembered from boyhood days right up to now. He surpassed himself. In that Heaven-sent relief, in an excess of creative virility he invented others, hurled them out into the scandalized night.

Out of breath he arose, thus barking his shin against the overturned chair. So he kicked the chair across the veranda. Swearing quite angrily he limped inside the humpy and lit the slush lamp. Yes! he *had* put the billy on, his one and only billy. And while he'd fallen asleep out on the veranda the fire had burnt the bottom out of it.

17

CARLSON'S AWAKENING

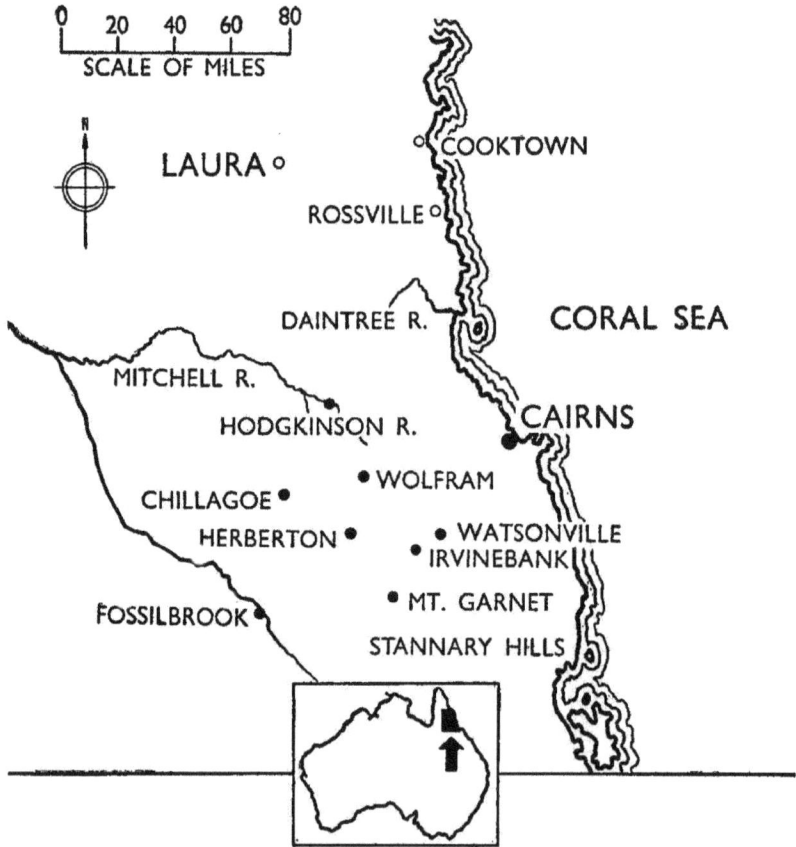

"I WONDER if Carlson was right!"

As I read over these faded lines, written on a North Queensland tin-field some forty years ago - I wonder. Especially in view of the fantastic scientific discoveries, biological as well as chemical, that have taught us so much since.

Anyway, this simple story was worked out among that maze of precipitous hills and gullies wherein venturesome prospectors found so many rich tin-fields just south of Cairns, Stannary Hills, Irvinebank, Herberton, Flaggy, Mount Garnet, and numerous smaller fields, some now forgotten under the ravages of time and closer settlement

Carlson, I had known before, when as a lad I carried my swag to Lightning Ridge, the black-opal fields of New South Wales. To meet him again, far to the north among the tin-fields scattered throughout that wonderland of the Cairns Tablelands and outlying ranges, seemed ordinary enough, for in those days we prospectors and "on our own" miners wandered far and wide at the call of fortune. Throughout every State, in fact, from Western Australia to the farthest north of Queensland, from Victoria to Tasmania, to New Zealand, to New Guinea, to wherever that voice called. Thus again I had met Carlson. With quiet smile and firm handshake he welcomed me.

I was but little more than a lad, he a quiet weather-beaten man fast going grey. His was a wealth of experience on mineral fields throughout the continent, which gave him fascinating topics of conversation. But his talk was not only of things seen and done, for he was one of those men whom we more happy-go-lucky fellows used to think of as "deep thinkers".

Often I would stroll across to Carlson's lonely camp and we would yarn by the campfire at night. Like so many of the bushmen who led the isolated lives of those years, Carlson had had plenty of time and opportunity, and the inclination, to think. Puffing a pipe under the stars by a lonely campfire at night offers a great inducement to "think things out".

And Carlson, as so many of the older hands, had often wondered at that ever-present mystery - Life and Death.

And herein is his theory of what would probably happen after death. I cannot give it to you in that quiet, drawly voice of his under the starlight with the campfire flames dancing on the tree-trunks. But his theory, in the old yellow notes now before me, is all here, I have tried to put his very own beliefs into what actually happened, if his beliefs were true.

Several years later, farther north in Cape York Peninsula, on the tin-fields back at Cooktown, I heard what had eventually happened to Carlson, so I wrote this, his story. I have tried to put it together exactly as it would have happened if his theory were correct.

And, as many believe now, the old bushman's idea could be so.

John Carlson toiled deep within the mountain. The ring of the hammer on the drill pierced the stillness just as thoughts pierced the silence of his mind. He put down his tools, musing. The enclosing granite loomed solid as the rock of ages. How futile! Immediately his insect-like tapping ceased, progress stopped. He was like someone searching for a needle in a haystack, but his task was far more difficult. For this haystack was a mountain of solid rock, the needle a lode of tin - somewhere.

Just like knowledge within the brain. It was there - somewhere. But immediately a man stopped thinking silence. And to think definitely and steadily to a successful issue was such laborious, long-drawn-out work. Again like looking for a needle in a haystack!

This mountain and a man's brain were fantastically alike. They were always silently there. Both contained wealth. To reach it a man must labour long in the dark - and then perhaps miss it.

Carlson reached for his pipe. The candle burned steadily. "Like a man's life," thought Carlson, "burning definitely to the end, quite irrespective of what he does. The time limit, with the man inside struggling for sweets like an ant in a syrup bowl."

Carlson lit up, sitting back against the rock-face. The mountain enclosing him seemed waiting, its silence power-fully urging him to think. "All in a circle, never getting nearer to what is in me, the Me of me. Now why *am* I here, isolated from everyone, and everything? I'm familiar with the prizes of life, and yet I've wilfully wasted my chances by living in these lonely places. And the most curious influence on my life is this particular mountain. I've come back here again and again, drawn by something I can neither understand nor resist. I'm striving for wealth. I feel certain it is here. Why? I don't know. Something tells me. What is Something, and why has it directed all my life? This last search has meant two years of animal-like toil, just boring further and further into darkness. Apparently I'll keep on seeking until the time limit douses my own light."

He put down his burnt-out pipe and began counting plugs of gelignite. He now had six deep holes bored in the face. With judicial plugging of the explosive, a shattering "blow-out" would result. "The triumph of mind over matter," he mused. "Dynamite will shift a mountain. If man could only invent a mental dynamite, to blow the cobwebs away and let him see what is really master inside of him! I don't want to waste all my life here, and yet my mind compels me stay. And the body, which is what I can see and apparently is so much the stronger, is completely bossed by the mind. And I, whatever I am, is the slave. Strikes me it's Kismet."

Half smiling, he charged the holes in the roof first, sliding four plugs into each, carefully tamping them until they were air-tight with loam. Then the holes in the "toe", well plugged and with their varying lengths of fuse. The longest he would light first, the shortest, last. Thus, when the last was lit, the first would have burnt to equal length, allowing him ample time to run down the tunnel to safety just before the charges would explode at their measured time.

Holding the muddy rammer, he paused, smiling at the blank granite wall facing him. "Silent as the Sphinx," he mused, "and knows as much. Only, the last was lit, the first would have burnt to equal length, allowing him ample time to run down the tunnel to safety just before the charges would explode at their measured time.

Holding the muddy rammer, he paused, smiling at the blank granite wall facing him. "Silent as the Sphinx," he mused, "and knows as much. Only, the Sphinx has expression. So has my face. But man gave the Sphinx expression. What gave me mine? And what is the Me behind the expression? I don't even know myself. This shot will break down *your* face, old rock, and may show me what I want to know behind it. It may uncover slabs of tin. I don't know what tin really is, but it means wealth. So here goes for your great awakening."

He held the candle to fuse after fuse, kneeling calmly while making sure each merrily hissed the sparks that spell no misfire. Fumes rapidly clouded the face as he turned to go. Ominous smoke from a "toe" hole made him pause. He had lit the last fuse first!

He leapt back to turn and run-three seconds later enveloped in a flame that wiped out the universe, not even hearing the thunderous roar, unaware of the shocking, tearing vibrations wrenching solid rock to whizzing fragments, shuddering the very heart of the mountain as if it were bursting, totally unaware of the sulphurous fumes, the red-hot grit, the galloping globes of flame as the searing blast roared down to the tunnel mouth to escape in rolling echoes down over the valleys.

Nature required three days for his violently ejected consciousness to reform. His deep belief had been that though you can smash a living thing to dust or ashes you cannot kill the Life that gave it being, that Life which in a human is a consciousness that causes it wonder at the sun and the moon and the stars, and the glee in a baby's eyes. You can never annihilate the Life. And in the absolute darkness, the strange, sighing quietness down there within the very womb of the mountain, this very thought reforming brought him his first glow of conscious triumph. He hovered quiescent while the threads of his mentality slowly, surely gathered into a coherent, conscious whole. "Like being born again, but how pleasantly, and surely, and-consciously. As I thought might be the Great Secret! But how inexpressibly more wonderful than the thought!"

And then - he could see! After it happened he realized he had subconsciously known he would, but the wonder of it when it was reborn within him - in a flash he knew it must be so, for sight was first given him untold thousands of years ago. But this sight was an incomparably more beautiful thing than all the many Sights he had known put together; never more would darkness or distance or fogs or rain dim *this* sight.

He was smiling then with a quiet sympathy, but understandingly, smiling down at the pulverized body lying grotesquely sprawled upon the tunnel floor. That had been *his*. Poor thing! And how he had cared for it, and how much trouble it had given him! What a weak, inefficient, highly vulnerable vessel to help nourish and develop this wonderful magic called Life! Still, it had served its purpose, done its best. It was the Me, his own consciousness hovering there that, day-dreaming a moment, had really been responsible for shattering that poor thing to pulp.

It looked an absurd thing now, sprawling there within its darkness, so obviously "dead", like an insect's discarded chrysalis. Wonderingly, in growing delight he examined his new form. Shaped like the old and feeling more substantial, though not of the flesh, he felt it radiating powers undreamt of by Earth Man.

He felt it had no weight, and was not chained by gravitation. He felt he could move it at a thought, and with the speed of thought should he wish. And now it dawned within him that his Earth Man's death had born him into some new and marvellous dimension in which space and time, material things and pain, speed and mass held no restrictions at all. Such ills or accidents as hurt an Earth Man were powerless to tarnish *this* body. But its consciousness was now swiftly entrancing him - this vibrant power of Life, unlimited vision, above all this unfolding understanding rapidly making him master of some concentrated knowledge of ages. Intuitively he realized he must now indelibly memorize the little knowledge gained in its earth life with the aid of that worked-out clay at his feet, that last shattered envelope lying sprawled so grotesquely before him. He knew now that the Past lives on in the Present. Anything of value he had ever learnt in any of his chain of lives had never been lost. It had been absorbed into the one spirit-memory, if not for use in that life, then in some other. And now all were merging together in this vibrant ultimate creation which was *he*.

He knew now that the only thing of value gained by that lifeless body in its lifelong struggles was a wisp of a something that cannot be seen, or weighed, or measured. A priceless, enduring, creative activity of life which each life crystallized into a shadow of understanding learnt from innumerable experiences, encased within imperishable memory. And that priceless wisp of ultimate reality was his! From out the chaotic dross of his many lives was now moulded this form, sublime, brilliantly alive in creative understanding, a human spirit slowly unfolding to dazzling secrets of the universe of which it had ever been and ever would be a generative part, but of which it was only now growing realistically aware.

He glanced at the dead man's work, with a friendly smile realizing that the poor uncouth human had done his work well, even though the one careless mistake had made it its last job. The face was a jumble of shattered rock, when cleaned up it would have advanced the tunnel by at least three feet, a good shot indeed in that tough rock. With a reminiscent thrill he further saw that but a foot deeper into the unblasted rock was the edge of a tinstone reef.

The man, after all, had been correct in his blind groping. With a sympathetic smile Carlson thought of the fortune that had been at last within grasp of that toiling human. How futile such fortune appeared now! As useless, as meaningless to such as he as a chest of gold would be to a fish.

Acting upon thought, Carlson sped up through the mountain, following the tin lode up to the surface. His body now was of a substance capable of penetrating what humans call solids, as electricity flows unhindered through copper, as radio waves fly through mountains. He emerged on the mountain summit amongst trees and sunlight, seeing that only a few feet of loam and mouldering leaves hid the cap of the tin lode from human vision. So that was why he had never found the lode! He and others had prospected over this summit a dozen times. Ah, but with *human* eyes!

Invisible to human sight he waited there, compelled to reconstruct the Past, connecting himself as a deathless link in the Universal Plan from the very Dawn of Man.

It was hard work, a work he had never experienced before. Gradually he felt the thrill growing sublime as his mentality began to do this, as if from some universal reservoir drawing understanding that he was an everlasting atom of Life intermingled with all in the universe.

The knowledge came at first as if hard drawn out of some vast, vast sleep. To realize gradually, in growing amazement, that he was drawing upon many lives, that this fast concentrating knowledge was coming from many experiences banked for him by Nature between many "sleeps", his previous lives on earth. When he had thought he had been fully alive he had not been even semi-conscious. Only now was he becoming alive, awake for the first time in a long stream of lives. In this his awakening, neither day nor night, nor time held meaning as it had in his human lives.

And now this ordinary mountain summit towered to a vast peak crowned with giant trees of gradually recognized foliage and strange, creepered plants with gigantic leaves which Carlson wonderingly remembered. At the tree roots there outcropped the black rocks of this tin lode, but what a mighty outcrop! A man pushed craftily through the undergrowth, lithe and noiseless in his bare brown feet, an animal skin girding his loins.

Carlson, though immeasurably superior in his new body, could not but admire the superb physical perfection of this untamed animal whose fiercely handsome face was framed with drooping black curls and beard. Carlson watched him as a scientist would study an interesting germ under a microscope.

The fellow listened, peering with splendid eyes, then, reassured, was about to pass on when something in the tin lode attracted his eye. He reached down, but, finding the specimen boulder too heavy, dropped his stone axe, heaved and wrenched the boulder away with an animal-like grunt. Carlson interestedly noted the object of the stone-age man's curiosity. It was not the tinstone, not the bunch of crystals even, but their sharp edge that intrigued him so. He broke off crystal after crystal, testing each one, only to desist disappointedly and pick up his weapon, running a loving thumb across its edge.

Carlson smiled sympathetically. The stone-age man had hoped that here was a source of already sharpened spear or tomahawk heads, only to prove the crystal too brittle. He must remain contented with the great labour of sharpening the hard flint stones until the development of human knowledge provided a solution. And that such a solution would be found was indicated by the man's own curiosity.

The man's disappointment shocked Carlson into the realization that he was spying on his own self of unknown thousands of years ago. This, then, explained why he had so obstinately searched for that tin! Never-dying memory had locked the knowledge of it away for reference in some far distant age - this present age.

Carlson stood there for long, as humans measure time, reconstructing his memories, forming each one with its knowledge gained into a compact entirety, gathering up his lives in a dazzling array of understanding until he began to glimpse the reason why man was born. He found the earth but a schoolhouse of Life, that he had been born and reborn for ages, and that not until he had accumulated a chain of memories that linked all the earth would he acquire the power to speed to other knowledge, maybe in this world, maybe in other worlds.

It was a glory, that job of tabulating his bygone experiences. Only now he reaped the fruits of knowledge gained as the arrogant captain of a Roman legion, tasted the bitterness of the downtrodden as a harassed Jew in a Russian slum. As an Armenian doctor he learnt what torture meant under the hands of the Turk, learnt the clean, sweet value of mercy. He had been a negro savage and a Chinese coolie, throughout thousands of toiling years he had accumulated, life by life, varied knowledge, until not one country in the world but had buried his bones after giving him life of memory.

A day came when with a detatched but delightful interest he watched a packhorse team struggling up the mountain slope, which now once more appeared to Carlson as it had in his latest life. At the summit, the horses shivered in wild-eyed alarm. With difficulty, the two men drove them past Carlson.

"What the blazes is the matter with the fools?" questioned one angrily. "Anyone would think they had seen a ghost!"

"Maybe they have," replied his mate soberly.

"What rot! I've known horses and dogs to play up like that at night now and then, but this is broad daylight! Well, let's have a pipe. It's a great view here. With that haze rolling among the peaks, it looks like some great old sea. I've never been here before, but. these big old hills do appear strangely familiar."

"Same here. I could have sworn I recognized landmarks as we climbed this old-man hill. And the more I see of it, the more I believe it is tin country."

"Yes I feel sort of confident, too, wish to goodness it proves right. Anyway, we can only try. We'll have the place much to ourselves. There's only one hatter hereabouts, so I've heard, some hermit chap named Carlson. His humpy is away down in the gorge somewhere. I wonder if he has found anything."

Carlson, listening intently, deliberately and easily used his new-born concentration of mind-power to insert into these men's minds the compelling thought to go and find and work his tunnel.

Presently the elder pocketed his pipe.

"What if we look for a way down into the gorge," he suggested dreamily, "and try find this fellow Carlson's camp? He may be a decent sort. Perhaps he might put us onto something."

"Right. Good idea."

Which is how one of the rich tin-mines in North Queensland was discovered, although the lucky prospectors will never dream the truth until they meet Carlson later.

It was days later in human time that Carlson, feeling within himself the power of a very god, sped upwards with the speed of thought.

18

ONE WILD AND WOOLLY CHRISTMAS
AT THE COEN

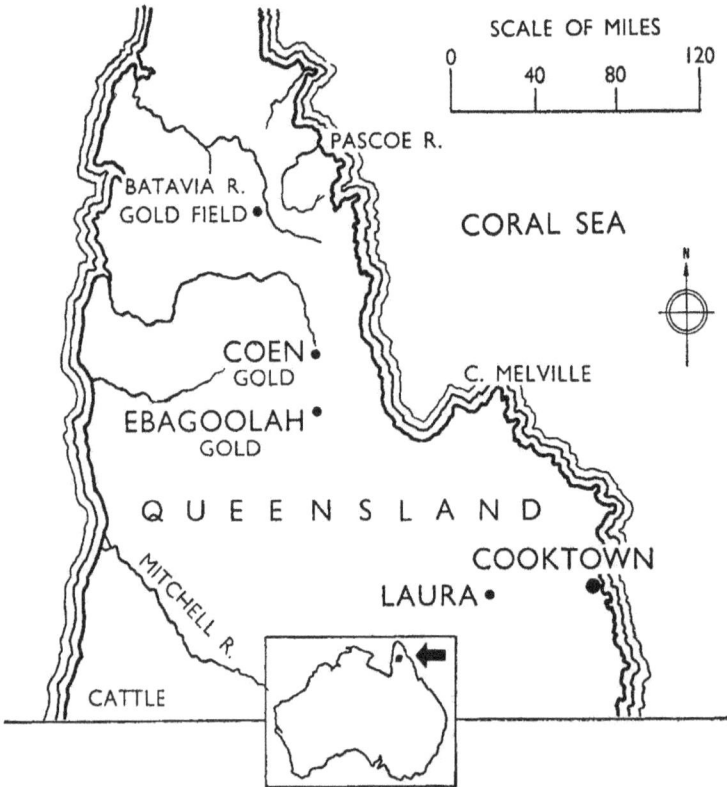

THIS vanished Christmas took place well before the discovery of gold at Portland Roads, which now makes the Coen accessible by sea. At this particular Christmas time it was only accessible by the long, lonely track cut up through the bush from Cook town to mark the way of the telegraph line which ended at extreme north near Torres Strait.

I realize, with something like a shock, that I have written of a phase of Australian bush life now fast vanishing. We never dreamt it would be so in those days, our familiar life seemed there to stay. The aboriginal tribesmen, who entered so much into life in the north, were plentiful then and still wild in localities, especially along the west coast. The hunt for gold.

The so few (barely half a dozen) pioneering cattle-stations. The sandalwood teams and the constant searching for the golden wood. The often overdue packhorse teams loaded with tucker before the Wet should set in. Our horses, our constant travelling through trackless bush. The tiny Coen which was the one "town" past Cooktown in the whole big Peninsula. Our occasional bouts of fever, the disaster when a valuable horse or two was speared, the swift whisper of "Gold!" - a rise in the price of sandalwood. News of a mate perished in the bush, maybe eaten by wild pigs. Or simply vanished. Killed by the blacks, or some accidental tragedy-we would never know. All these happenings were in a familiar life that appeared set to stay for a century ahead.

And soon now Man will be flying to the moon. The pace is fast - I wonder where it is taking us!

The picturesque Coen is an Australian Bret Harte mining camp. Set in a grassy amphitheatre among granite hills, its sixty iron houses are grouped companionably together. It nestles in the centre of Cape York Peninsula.

Southward lie two hundred miles of wild bush right to Cooktown, while north is two hundred miles of much wilder bush, which terminates at Endeavour Strait. The tiny place exists in an atmosphere of carefree isolation. At Christmas, Coen is "the world". I saw my most memorable Christmas there.

A week beforehand the Peninsula crowd had begun to roll up for the yearly "cash in". Numbers had ridden over two hundred miles, from north, east, south, and west. There were bushmen from the Laura, morose hatters from the Batavia River diggings, sluicers from Cannibal Creek, fossickers from the Pascoe, cattlemen even from the Mitchell and the Gulf country.

An open-hearted crowd, but tough! Sandalwood-getters, prospectors, cattlemen, tin-scratchers, nomads, and men whose object in existence was a masterless time of hardship and romance. All carried arms, generally a holstered revolver at the saddle, for in the farthest north the blacks in places were by no means safe.

Deeply sunburnt men all, clear of eye, dressed in breeches and open-necked shirt or sleeveless flannel. Tall men, short men, wiry men, but all strong chaps, used to working hard on salt beef and damper. Some were clean-shaven, but most wore a moustache, and numbers a beard. The greybeards amongst them were as lively as crickets, each quite obviously considering himself as good a man as any there. All were in the humour for a lively Christmas, and they wasted no time in stepping on it. The supply lugger from Cooktown had arrived at Port Stewart, and the straggling pack-horse team, tired and dusty after their forty-mile climb, were trailing into camp. "Port Stewart", by the way, is an iron shed set upon a mud bay.

The first day's greetings absorbed the beer, which, after all, was merely an appetizer and a luxury. Sixty horses cannot carry much beer, but they can transport whisky and rum sufficient for a battalion.

You see, there was nothing else to do. And everyone did it.

The second day ended with the crowd nicely "set", shouting a hilarious send-off to the supply team *en route* to the "Port" for a second loading.

That night was peaceful in its stars. The mountain threw slumbrous shadows over the tiny town. Revelry rang from the pub, all lit up by hurricane lamps along the veranda. The boards were creaking to heavy feet as men rollicked and sang to "buck sets". Three fiddles and four concertinas rattled out the happy old-time tunes.

"Tame" natives were grouped along the veranda edge, their eyes gleaming with enjoyment of the frolic of their masters. Down Pannikin Creek way came sounds of a wild hullabaloo as the clashing of nullahs kept time to the stamping of feet and fierce, animal-like grunts where the local tribe celebrated Christmas in their own way.

But on the veranda those not actually dancing were hanging over the bar or sprawled on the grass outside, exchanging reminiscences with new-found mates. Wondrous tales, strangely enough mostly true ones, of patches of sandalwood found down towards the unknown west coast where the "niggers" are hairy as animals and twice as wild, tales of gold from that queer Batavia diggings northward, tales of tin streamed in tons, galloping tales of scrubbers and cattle, tales of romance and of money to burn.

And we knew there was no boasting, for the Sandalwood Kings had hundreds of pounds in their kick, while on the liquor-slopped bar there glistened entrancing nuggets from Batavia, and on the grass outside, spilt carelessly on chaff-bags, were shammies of "shotty" gold, with serious-visaged men appraising the weight by hand "for drinks".

So the night wore on, unobtrusively, like Time.

Next day was "niggers' day", for everyone had one or more tame native horse-boys; each Sandalwood King had a dozen. The men congregated there represented ownership of well over a thousand horses. The prospectors' "boys" had in some cases been faithful for years, braving wild blacks, fire, flood, starvation, and all hardships with their masters.

So all day long were races, foot and horse, the native competitors showing the keenest rivalry, combined with a hair-raising skill. Later there were boxing tournaments in which the natives were blindfolded, then their gloves substituted for bags filled with flour. The bags were pricked, the natives first pushed at one another then away they went hammer and tongs.

The vim with which they plastered each other's blackness with flour was a sight hilariously greeted by white and black alike. At one stage of the combats twenty "boys" were in action simultaneously. The flour was a shameful waste, but - it was Christmas.

Inevitably that night the talk was all of "boys". Each man had a wonderful boy, or had had a prodigious boy. His particular boy possessed those priceless points usually attributable to the whitest white men.

Old Sandy Graham had a boy in whom was combined all the virtues of a paragon. Tears streamed into Sandy's whiskers as he shouted praise of that marvellous boy of his; but no one would listen, all had boys of their own to talk of, while even the non-drinkers obviously would not take old Sandy quite seriously. He glared around, searching for an audience, but the rest of the chaps were singing with the light-hearted abandon of voices that only tasted song once in twelve months.

Old Sandy was thoroughly exasperated. Howling that he would bring the boy right here and force the whole crowd to drink his health, he roared his way outside, packed his saddle-bags with bottled rum, mounted unsteadily, and rode off.

The following day was a little livelier. A hundred Pannikin Creek natives congregated warily near the hostelry, ready to run at first sight of a practical joker. Rifles were erratically cracking as uncertain but willing marksmen shot for drinks for the crowd. The target was an empty rum-bottle on a distant stump; but the tame natives refused to place the bottles after one exuberant marksman had fired a magazine at their heels to "see 'em corroboree".

Any unwary bird that Hew over the pub attracted a fusillade of revolver shots, with a following roar of laughter as it volplaned for the scrub. A bullet or two accidentally pierced an iron roof, which would soon have to be mended when the Wet season set in.

So the days and nights passed snappily, each bringing its own surprising variety, until Christmas Day. Some day I will write up that particular day. I may not be believed, but then it took me some time to believe it myself.

I have a hazy recollection of eventide, when the tame natives screamed news of Sandy's return. Shortly afterwards came his howling welcome, accompanied by the thunder of his horse's hooves on the veranda. The neddy plunged on the boards and snorted at the bar door but Sandy overcame his shyness with blows from an empty rum-bottle and the prad bounded in amongst us, to Sandy's triumphant roar, "The best -- nigger in the Peninsula, boys! Drink his health, he's dry as the hobs o' Hades!"

We gazed in a petrified silence. Sandy held a native slung across his saddle, but such a native! No wonder half the company stared in a questioning dismay. Even the barmen rubbed their eyes, and they were only half a bottle a day men. Then a long, lanky cattleman guffawed almost hysterically, and I knew I hadn't got 'em after all.

For the native Sandy carried was smoke-dried. It was a shrivelled caricature of death, the protruding bones hideous under blackened skin. Its matted hair fringed down to glaring eyes of red-walnut pods red-ochred. The nose cavity was plugged with fire-baked clay; the teeth grinned from smoke-shrunken lips.

It was a smoke-dried mummy. Odd tribes up north preserve their dead that way.

Sandy spurred his terrified horse to the bar and tipped off his load. The horse tipped Sandy off, and plunged like a thunderstorm through the door. Sandy fell with a resounding wallop. The mummy struck the bar like wood. It was very light, but hard as ironbark.

When Sandy finished swearing he staggered to the bar, affectionately propped the corpse against a demijohn, and roared: "There y'are, boys! You know Split-nose, the cutest boy ever bred in the Peninsula, bar none. The slickest cattle-thief ever born - worked fer me fer sixteen years! Some sneakin' brute put a bullet in 'im jest after we left 'ere last Christmas. If I could only find the cove I'd send 'im where Split-nose 'as gone. Drink to 'im boys, a real white man under a black 'ide, gone where we all must go."

We drank to the honour of Split-nose, best boy ever bred in the Peninsula, while the deceased cattle-thief crouched propped up on the bar, leering at us through the tobacco smoke. Little wonder that that Christmas at the Coen produced a record crop of the horrors.

19

THE LUCK OF FENG LI CHOO

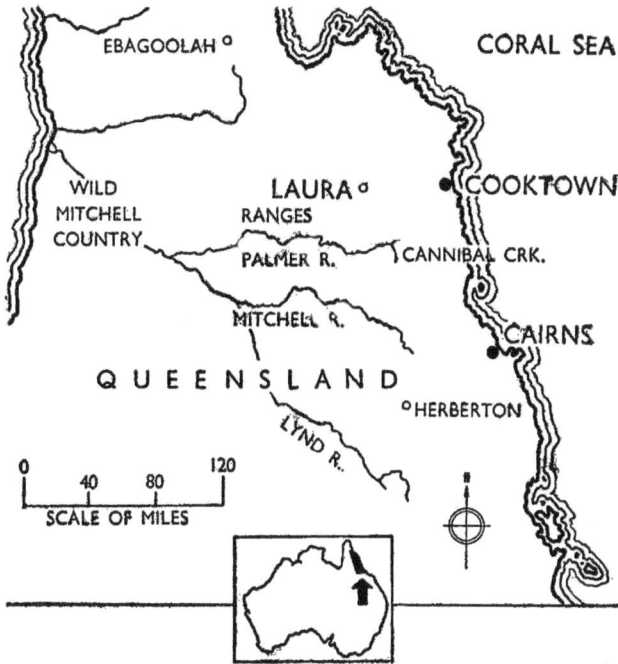

Now, a bushman is hardly less superstitious than his fellow townsman. I suppose we all have our private beliefs in "good luck" charms and tokens and talismans and all that sort of thing. But in the silent spaces many things could be possible that would appear absurd to the hemmed-in life of the town. It is the loneliness, I suppose; perhaps the way a man thinks, thinking, thinking, until all things look really possible. Perhaps it is the wideness of everything. Or the height of the stars in the sky. I don't know.

Anyway, when two years of gruelling luck have dragged a man close to despair, he is liable to clutch at any queer straw.

A Queensland night, stars in a velvet sky. The lowlands shadowed by sombre mountains. Over all, that brooding stillness of the far North.

Abruptly - it was sacrilege - there squeaked a medley of discordant sounds. A Chinese fiddle.

I turned to the old tin prospector smoking by the hut fire. "What a hideous row! Do you suffer it often, Don?"

"Must, lad," drawled the ancient. "Can't stop it, the Chinks are eighty to six here."

The fiddle ceased. The night dreamed again.

Through the open door tinkled real music to the bushman-horse-bells as the neddies cropped grass.

This was Cannibal Creek, a forgotten tin-mining camp in the Byerstown Ranges, one hundred miles towards the Palmer side of Cooktown. The wild Palmer blacks had eaten twenty Chinamen within fifty yards of old Don's hut. But since then other Chinamen had come, had persisted, were still there.

My mate Harry and I, travelling "bush" in the middle of a hard-luck prospecting trip, had located the isolated camp that afternoon. And now old Don was telling us all about this Feng Li Choo and his "lucky idol". We had heard the familiar tale before, told round campfires from Cooktown to Ebagoolah.

Old Don stared thoughtfully at the fire.

"Well, lads," he said deliberately, "it's only superstition."

But the fact is that Feng Li Choo is the luckiest man in this ten thousand square miles of country. His luck is uncanny, real supernatural. He's always had the richest claim, always found the richest patches of tin in this creek. Everything big has always been located by Feng. Even when the pack-team takes his tin to Cook town his luck goes with it, because for all these years he has always struck the highest market. He's never sold on a low market yet. His luck holds out in everything. He always gets the pick of the native women, always the strongest workers among the men.

"It was the Chinee packer who first blabbed the yarn of the idol, while I was dosing him with quinine when he was delirious with fever. It appears that in the last of the Palmer days a Chinee priest of some kind came to the great rush, having made a vow never to return home until he'd dug up enough gold to rebuild the temple of some favourite god.

"He struck gold in dishfuls on the Palmer, like many another blooming Chink; they called him the Golden Chow. But his luck deserted him the very night he was to leave with his gold for China, his team of Chinee carriers waiting, all loaded up.

"He was so elated at being able to keep his vow and so get a sure ticket to Paradise that at the send-off feast he got hilariously drunk on Chinee wine, and took a pretty half-caste girl. That finished him, like many other better men.

"It appears a woman was against the rules and regu¬lations of his order. Anyway, next morning he was down with raging fever. The carriers bolted with the gold, but whites and browns and blacks and yellows were pretty wild in those roaring times, and I don't think many of the runaways got away with it.

"Feng Li Choo nursed the priest, so in gratitude, I suppose, he gave Feng a joss that he'd carried all the way from the temple, explaining that so long as the joss was with him Feng would have unceasing luck, providing he took the joss back to its old home in the temple when his fortune was made. If he didn't, then devils would sprout in his liver and chew it day and night."

"Feng didn't stick on at the goldfield?" queried Harry.

"No," replied Don, "he came here, bringing his devil's luck with him. The Chinkies say he is returning to China soon, to build a new temple, then settle down as a mandarin. I wonder he's not gone home years ago, considering the coin he's amassed."

"Do you think there's anything in it - about the joss bringing a man luck if he is looking for gold, I mean?" asked Harry sheepishly.

Don smiled. "You're looking for gold, aren't you?" he said with a twinkle. "Well, you boys just test it. If you steal the joss, Feng will knife you sure, and I'll jump his claim when he clears out!"

Harry and I were not much more than kids, and we could not resist the temptation to stickybeak around Feng Li Choo's claim next morning. It was rich. We had never seen anything so rich in alluvial tin before. It was a little fortune. Yet other men had worked that ground and hardly made tucker before Feng came along with his lucky joss.

That night was black as Sheol. After the fiddle had ceased its nervy screech, I peered through the one tiny chink in the Chinaman's hut.

Upon the earthen floor on his knees he was, forehead bowed to the ground, arms in obeisance, muttering fervently in Chinee. Sandalwood tapers burnt with cloying incense from a dragon-painted jar. On a box before him, upon a plush stool, squatted a tiny joss.

I could not see it distinctly in that shadowed slush light, but its colour was purple like the sheen on choice grapes. With arms folded upon its lap it sat. Feng Li Choo's devotion was sincere and long. He put his bowed body into it and his soul shone from his almond eyes.

Reverently he arose, cleaned his hands, and bedded the joss in a cunning hole in the earthen floor, dragging a bag of tin over it. I sneaked away.

We mustered the horses next morning, then had breakfast. It was a simple plan, though we both smoked the pipes of excitement; even our old dog seemed uneasy.

When the Chinaman left for work we would pack our neddies, purloin the joss, then vanish. If this joss would bring us luck in our search for gold then we would idolize it. We would return it - some day.

Scoundrels? Granted. The Chinamen by law were not supposed to be mining there. But then there is no law in that great untamed Peninsula, hence how could we come under a law? Our own moral law? Alas, there is no law so immoral as the Law of Gold.

Feng Li Choo padded to his daily toil. We allowed him half an hour to get settled, then quickly packed the two old horses. They were our all. Those two cunning stagers for years past had packed our tools and tucker many hundreds of miles over plain and bush and mountain, while Harry and I tramped stubbornly along behind.

I hurried to Feng's hut. Harry brought the horses along, his eyes big and questioning. He carried the rifle, too, I saw with doubt. An excitable boy doing wrong with a rifle in his hand-tragedy might result.

The hut was muggy inside, Chinese eating things were stacked neatly along the walls, but the corner where the joss was hid smelt mildewy and somehow Oriental. I man-handled the bag of tin and reached straight down into that noisome hole - my guardian angel must have impelled me to snatch back my hand!

I struck a match - and peered into the half-closed, beady eyes of a death-adder.

I lost my very breath in those icy seconds, my heart stopped and I sprang round and faced Feng Li Choo. His eyes gleamed more cruelly than the adder's and his face showed no mouth as we crashed to the floor in the delirious reaction of fight.

Had Harry not come I would have killed him. I was mad after the fright. He fought like a beast, snarling, kicking, biting.

We lashed him to his own bunk, twisted a towel over his mouth, searched his writhing body, and found the joss strapped against his middle.

His eyes were all hate as Harry killed the adder.

We travelled fast throughout that day and evening, with many a backward glance, many a listening even after the stars had come. At late night we camped on the Palmer, allowing the horses to snatch a bellyful of grass, then pressed on into the dawn. Cold it was, and the shadows of the trees seemed moving. We turned and twisted and broke across into Campbell Creek, and all next day urged the horses on into the rugged Palmer Ranges, covering our tracks with all our knowledge of bushman ship. For three days and nights we travelled over some of the roughest country in Cape York Peninsula; then, where the ranges meet as solid walls of rock at the head of the great creek we halted in safety, anxious to prospect the promising-looking country round about.

The sun shone so cheerfully in the morning that we tried the "luck" of the joss. I remember a blue-striped jackass disdainfully watching us from a dead tree branch as Harry dug a dishful of wash-dirt from in under the creek-bank. My heart accompanied those wild pick strokes, but Harry was actually sweating.

"Now we'll try this old joss out." He grinned, but a fever of expectancy shone from his big brown eyes.

I stood by like a cat on hot bricks while he washed the prospect, half dreading the result. I confess an uncanny faith in the joss had grown on us during those few hurrying days, the damn thing seemed to have imbued us with a terrible confidence.

Harry shouted hysterically as a half-ounce piece gleamed partly buried in the dish. How it shone - oh Heavens, how our hearts thumped! The first piece of gold for the last twelve months!

In exultant haste we tore into that bank, gouging for the wash-dirt, knocking the dish over in wild excitement. I sat the joss on a granite rock overlooking Harry as he panned the prospects and Harry laughed in reply to the benign smile of the squatting thing. It was a modelling in burnt clay, the delicate face patient with an expression as elusive as the stars. The sun sheened his purple cloak with a gleam rivalling our gold. We laid the gold on the cold grey rock before his squatting feet and he smiled, to our delight, a mocking smile.

Knocking off when it grew too dark to work, we weighed the gold. Twenty ounces - £80! More by far than we had won in the last twelve months.

No wonder we made that evening one joyous laugh and could not keep our eyes off the joss as the firelight danced on his purple. His wise, calm face smiled into the night as he must have smiled at the nights of a thousand years. Our old dog crouched beside us, cold nose on forepaws, gazing solemnly up at the joss.

We slept with him jealously treasured between us. An uneasy sleep it was, feverish with gold and purple and a Chinaman's blazing eyes. We each clasped a rifle. We would have shot any man who sought to steal our joss.

Next day we won fifteen ounces, and the very bush smiled. How different it was to the frown of the last two years, even the birds seemed to know.

The luck didn't last. On the third night there came a rifle shot - the mountains thundered - another shot - the ranges echoed and re-echoed.

Harry thrust the joss within the breast of his shirt. We listened, eyes straining through the night, the dog with his ears pricked, eyes wide awake. Silence-no sign of anything.

We watched until dawn, then Harry sneaked to the creek for water. I raced towards his startled shout. At the waterhole lay our two old neddies, shot through the head.

Harry raved. He loved those horses, willing friends through years of wandering. And more - without horses to carry our tools and food we were helpless. We were marooned, surrounded by barren, uninhabited ranges.

We spied tracks in the sandy creek, but lost them when they climbed a rocky ridge. We set the dog on the tracks, but they vanished in running water. We hurried back towards camp, determined that after breakfast we would carry a supply of food, comb both banks of the creek, pick up the tracks where our enemy had emerged from the water, and track him to the finish.

"He won't leave the vicinity while we hold the joss," breathed Harry vengefully.

The camp had been ravaged! The flour-bag had been emptied over the ground, our last tin of syrup had been tomahawked, ants were already thickly bogged in the mess, others were hurrying to the feast. In cursing fury we scraped up what we could, fried some sandy johnny-cakes, and gulped breakfast. Fools, they say, seldom think. We did - later.

Just when we were ready to start after our quarry Harry sagged to the ground, looking startled.

"What on earth is the matter?" I asked. But my mate sprawled over on his side, helplessly clawing the grass, fear on his face.

Even as I watched, strength seemed to ooze away from me. It was not painful, it was a more frightening feeling than that, like a man losing balance to be left on his head in the air.

For an hour we lay, powerless even to speak, but able to think-very hard. And the old dog licked my face, then Harry's.

What had the Chinaman put in the food? Why didn't he come? What would he do when he did come? Ugh! Those ants, swarming in a fighting brown mass over the spilt syrup!

He came, he shot our dog! Then he glared at us with the face of a gambler who had staked his all. In frenzied eagerness he clawed open Harry's shirt - and clutched the joss with a sob of joy.

His face all crinkled in smiles, he kissed his joss; in tender solicitude he sat it upon a pack-saddle, sank on his knees, bowed his forehead to the ground, and yabbered a fervent devotion, watered with real tears. His long plaited pigtail fell over his shoulder; the long, coarse black hair reminded me of our dead horses' tails.

The joss seemed pleased in his purple. I envied the calm of that image. I wished I could smile as it did. Lovingly Feng Li Choo put him away within his flannel shirt.

Then he rose, and gazed down at us with a slow, mirthless smile. He gazed quite a time, he seemed pleased at the look in our eyes. Then from my own belt he stole the pouch, the little fat pouch that held our gold. I tried to snap at his skinny wrist. He smiled, he nodded understandingly as he spilt the yellow stream into a pannikin. He balanced it appraisingly for our approval before he strapped the gold within his shirt beside the joss.

Feng kicked Harry for pleasure; he grasped him by the ankles and dragged him a little distance from me. A splintered stake caught in Harry's ear and tore it. Feng seemed pleased, he watched musingly while the blood dribbled on the white granite sand.

Then from the wreck of our corned beef he sliced tiny strips of meat. And I wondered - and wondered - and felt sick, and did not believe.

Feng Li Choo shuffled up the hilly bank to a nest of big red meat-ants. He laid a meandering trail with the meat, from the nest along to Harry. I was too sick to wonder any more. He laid another trail to me, dropping a piece here and a piece there amongst the grass. I was slightly closer to my ants than Harry was to his, but I understood why the Chinaman had smiled at Harry's bleeding ear.

Feng Li Choo speculatively eyed his handiwork. He seemed to think Harry had too much of a start, for he put a twist in the trail of meat that would lead the ants to me. Then he smiled down at us. He had no need to say a word. I closed my eyes. He was gone when I opened them to the blazing sun.

The ants nosed along from the nests - a few scouters.

As they hurried back my hair stood on end. Others came! Then streams of them. They swarmed. They reached Harry first!

A wandering band of Palmer natives saved us. They threw sand on us and shouted and stamped us all over with big bare feet before running us down to the creek and dumping us in the waterhole. It was the quickest way. Next morning our strength had returned. We gave the complete camp to the natives. They could have speared us the day before had they wished. We set out before we should see them eating our horses. We had a two-hundred-mile walk to Cooktown. It mattered little that we carried hardly any food.

I hate the sound of a Chinee fiddle.

20

THE SANDALWOOD-GETTERS

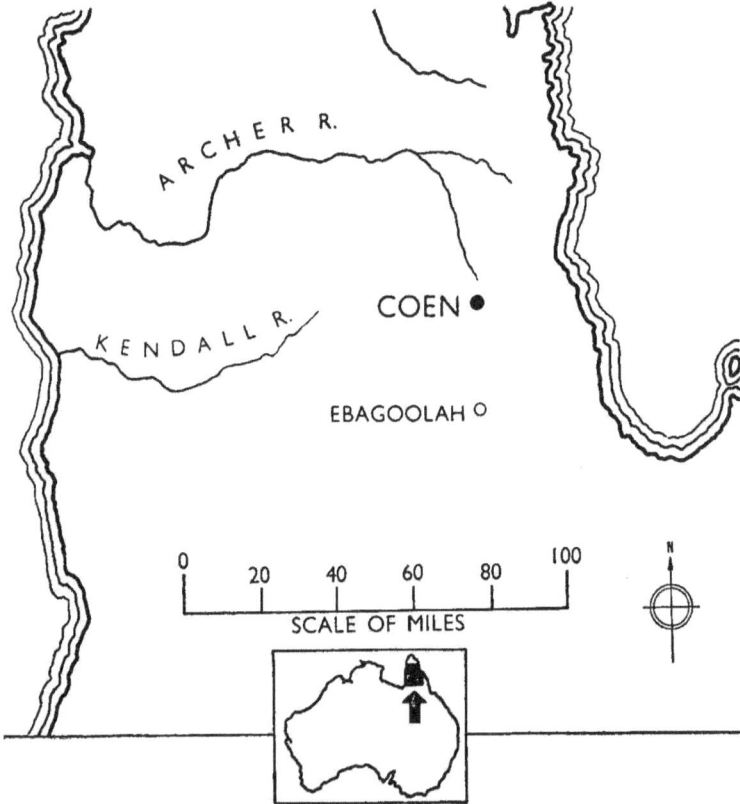

THIS story is merely an incident in the life of the sandal-wood-getters of Cape York Peninsula. The same kind of thing happened also three thousand miles to the west along the Western Australian coast before the sandalwood was cut out there. Throughout the Peninsula it was the favourite method of hostile natives. when they seized their war spears and went looking for trouble-which they did quite enthusiastically at times, before the two terrible Spanish influenza plagues practically wiped the poor folk out. This little incident of my earlier roaming days, though lively and interesting to me at the time, seemed so trivial in story form that I was going to tear it up. But the thought came that it is a very little known phase of Australian pioneering life that will never come again. So it goes on record for you, and future generations.

The pack-team mooched contentedly along, Long Andy with Travers and the blackboy Billy riding ahead. Carelessly riding midway along the team were Harry and Charlie, laughing for laughing's sake, as only blackboys can. The leading horses' rumps hunched solidly square as they braced themselves before disappearing down a creeper-matted ravine.

Away back, Silent Jim and I brought up the "railers". I turned in the saddle and gazed far away back. Nestling way down among the waves of mountains gleamed the roofs of little Coen, Cape York Peninsula's township of sandalwood and gold. Then a peak intervened, and I faced towards the west again.

We were travelling for sandalwood. The Coen natives had spoken of an unknown river on whose banks grew the golden trees, some distant stream running between the Archer and the Kendall, on the west coast of the Peninsula which is one of the last strongholds of the blacks. Most of its river-mouths are charted, though some mainly by guesswork. The country's reputation is of the blackest.

We toiled on for a while among the mountains, then began the long trek down the foothills through picturesque granite gorges, across ravines and wild creeks whose falling waters sing and weep over glistening black rocks. As the days drifted by, away below us the country spread almost flat to dim in haze-clouds towards the coast; it appeared as a straw-coloured sea from the miles of blady grass. Running down through it in parallel lines stood out many dark-green ribbons of scrub-flanked waterways.

Leaving the foothills behind, we ploughed through massed grasses. And right there the blackboys became uneasy for, much against their will, we were penetrating into the wild myall country. We slashed our way through the scrub on the banks of many creeks that feed the Kendall, then made across country for the Archer. If that alleged river ran in between, then we must strike it.

From an ironwood ridge, Silent Jim eventually spied the hoped-for stream. Just a column of trees floating down from the ranges to merge in flat country towards the coast. Here and there the sun gleamed on waterholes. Before we hit the river trees Charlie laughed and pointed. Three low, shrubby trees with lightish leaves and coarse bark. Sandalwoods! As we searched the bank we sighted many trees, laughing as we pointed them out to one another and breathed that husky feeling of gladness which grips men when they sense triumph.

Before us a couch-grass slope gently led to the water's edge. The leading horses shuffled quickly along. Couch is great feeding stuff and soon the neddies would be out of the heart-breaking blady grass, deadening stuff to force their hooves through.

The sweet grass bend was soon loud with two score horse-bells, the first civilized music those trees had ever heard. Soon they were to tremble to another tune - the ringing of the axes.

Charlie took the billies and slipped down for water. He shouted excitedly, pointing to the sand.

"Thought so." Long Andy grinned. "Native tracks! The boys'll have the wind up now. But we've got 'em so far from their own country that they'll be scared to run away."

Charlie wore a solemn look as he came hurrying back with the water. "Plenty wild fella blackboy sit down longa here," he said uneasily. "Me think it better pack up! Go back longa Coen quick-fella!"

"Yah!" grunted Long Andy. "Put on the billy an' we'll have some scran."

By evening we'd rigged camp with the big pack-saddles so arranged on poles that they'd afford shelter in view of an unheralded flight of spears. You take no chances on the West Coast.

The nights were beautiful. The circle of trees seemed always to be listening and whispering. The quiet water mirrored the pale gold of stars and the red of our cheerful fire. The bells tinkled. It was good to be alive.

After breakfast Travers, Billy, and I saddled up and spurred our unwilling prads back into the tall, sharp bladed grasses. We were to chum up with the wild natives if possible. They had a camp close by, their tracks were everywhere. If we could hire them to cut for us, then so much the better, very much so. If not, then we wanted to be left in industrious peace.

With uneasy instinct, Billy guided us to a swamp some miles away. Before reaching it we heard behind us the first sound of axes on the river-bank by our camp.

We sniffed smoke in the still air and spied behind a rampart of buffalo grass some eighty gunyahs, built of plaited reeds. A coil of carpet snake in a cooking fire's ashes advertised a breakfast suddenly interrupted. Several spear bundles left erect before gunyahs told convincingly of hurried flight.

These weapons were nasty-looking, the mortised hafts nine feet long, the barbs of jagged kangaroo bone or chipped quartz. The cooking utensils were of bark, with knives of 'roo bone and stone. A dozen rudely fashioned stone tomahawks lay beside a heap of stone chips. Their seed-grinders were of roughly hollowed stone.

Eighty gunyahs, with say four to each gunyah, meant a tidy lot of them. There was plenty of game in this country.

I peeped within a gunyah to sight the ugliest thing on earth. What had once been a face wasn't wrinkled, because the creases had mummified into corrugated parchment stretched tightly over bones. One eye was like a blob of greenish water dimly seen within a murky well. What molars she sported had long been ground level with the jaws. A wisp of greasy white hair sprouted on the otherwise naked skull. Strips of withered skin had once been breasts.

"Is it alive?" asked Travers incredulously.

"Yes," I said. "Sling the old lady a stick of 'bacca."

We planted a green bough in the centre of the camp and made a pile of tobacco, flour, and sugar, unmistakable sign of peace and trade.

I kept a sharp look-out over the thick grass tufts as we rode back, but that didn't prevent Travers's horse from screaming. I turned as he reared, the whites of his brown eyes bulging from their sockets. A spear-haft swayed from his back behind the saddle. I yelled to the spurring Billy to come back and fired into the grasses as the stricken horse went down. When natives have never heard rifle-fire they fear it as the angry voice of the thunder god.

Travers jumped for my stirrup iron, and we beat it. But never a sign of a native. We hit camp in time for dinner. Billy immediately communicated his fear to the other boys. Strange how scared natives are of natives!

After that, Silent Jim was installed as cook and camp guard, with Billy as horse-boy. We took no revenge for the slaughtered horse, though we did grudge him to them, especially since they ate him. We left their camp strictly alone, hoping they would do the same by us. Silent Jim as camp guard would take no chances; we could not afford to. This was a good patch of trees, we should soon cut enough wood to load the team. Night and day we constantly had to keep an eye on those precious horses. Within a fortnight we had cut and stacked six tons of the yellow wood handy to the camp. Thousands of pounds' worth are shipped yearly to China from Cooktown and Thursday Island. The shrewd Chinese extract the sandalwood oil and turn the scented wood into fancy boxes and so on to sell back to Australia and the world.

One scorching afternoon we were cutting about a mile up the river, dry grass-dust settling on our sweating bodies and torturing them as we trampled round the trees. A breeze sprang up about four o'clock. Long Andy straightened his back.

"Thank the Lord for that," he growled, "although it does feel as if it was blowing off a furnace."

Our blackboys ceased chopping, sniffing the air. The whites gleamed under Charlie's eyes.

Me smellem grass burn," he said excitedly. "Thinkim myall nigger fire 'im grass. Burn us up altogether!" Which startled us by its now obvious truth.

Quickly the sun was blotted out by billowing smoke, weirdly vivid with columns of flame. The earth hummed to a crackling roar. Dense timber a hundred yards thick lined the river-bank and from behind it, galloping parallel in the shallow water channel jangled the rollicking clangour of horse-bells - the bright-faced camp-boy was running the horses down to the waterhole. As we sighted the camp we saw fresh flames. Silent Jim at the run, trailing blazing bark, was firing the grass back from the camp.

From the main fire flat sheets of flame were being blown yards ahead. They licked the grass, and up leapt crackling tongues of scarlet. Flame sheets spattered against the ragged tea-trees and instantly the oily-barked branches were crawling with fire.

Just ahead of the inferno darted scores of brown hawks, scoffing up the swarms of grasshoppers and flying insects that scudded from the blaze. Birds, singly, in agitated pairs, and in droves, swished by in the scorching haze overhead.

Well back through the grass we ran in parallel lines to the camp, each man trailing strands of tea-tree bark whose pathway was instantly a wake of fire.

When the heat became unbearable we caved in. Our own fire burnt to the camp edge, unwillingly dying out. But it had made a break two hundred yards in depth between the camp and the advancing inferno.

Badly scared, Billy called out that the bank behind the camp was alive with blacks. We emptied our rifles among the trees, not wishing the horses to be speared as we drove them into the waterhole. They stood quietly in the water, necks held high, staring with big, inquiring eyes at the rolling wave of flame tearing riverwards. Their nostrils sniffed the acrid air, their bodies already covered with a coat of grey ash.

Along with the breeze floated a peculiar, pungent scent, which made Long Andy rage and curse.

"Never mind," said Silent Jim, "the big heap here is safe."

It was our precious sandalwood stacks burning along the river that made Andy mad. The oil-saturated wood burns as a heavy incense. Hundreds of pounds going up in smoke! A roar as of stampeding cattle heralded an eerily beautiful sight, a hundred head of wild horses galloping out of the smoke. Their leader a splendid stallion, with the ashes off his rounded back would have been a silver-grey. His arched neck and wonderful eyes told that this day he'd led in a race for life to save his mob. Close behind his flying hoofs galloped the mob, the rear brought up by slobberingly anxious mares hurrying along their foals.

They wheeled to the opening and thundered down the slope past the tent, and our horses instantly broke into excited neighing of welcome. The waterhole was churned into foam as the two mobs united.

The flames reached the green river trees and, there being no more grass to feed on, died down. We spent a brisk half-hour kicking singed reptiles out of the camp.

Silent Jim sought to console Long Andy.

"We're not too badly off," he drawled, "we've saved six tons of wood. When we left the Coen it was worth forty pounds a ton. We've got our own hides intact, and we've only lost one horse. We can pack the wood to Coen and come back with a stronger party. We're really on velvet. How about putting the billy on?"

"The wood's all damn well burnt," snarled Long Andy.

21

THE RIDE OF BRANNIGAN'S MEN

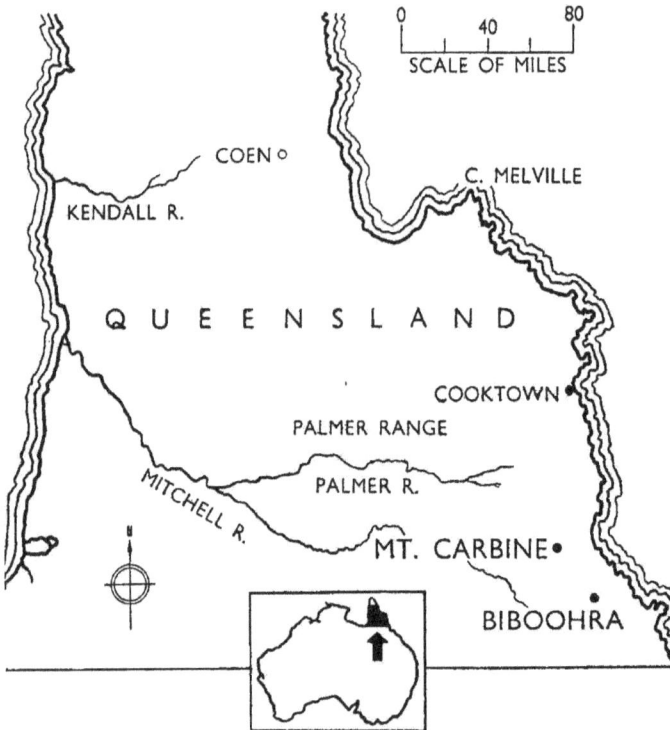

ALTHOUGH Cape York Peninsula, because of its far smaller area, isolation, and near inaccessibility, has never grown the vast herds of the Gulf Country, still the handful of pioneer stations have had to keep a wary look-out for the cattle-duffer. Here is a description of a well-planned raid on a large scale that just failed to come off. Only because of the quick wits of a half-wild aboriginal who, being hunted as a notorious cattle-spearer, saw his chance of wiping out his "crimes" and "getting in good" with the whites.

This is how, at no little risk to himself, he succeeded.

On a wild-eyed chestnut, Red Burke rode at the head of the mob, eyes piercing the moon-thrown shadows of tree and gully, ears alert for any sound that was not the swiftly-moving hoofs behind the clashing of horns, the nasty, half-grunting bellowings of fright.

A lively man on each flank, two hounding the rear.

A mob of three hundred fat steers worth a tenner a head at the Biboohra meatworks, three hundred miles down the great lonely Peninsula. Uninhabited country when once through the Kendall Gorge:

Womera Jimmy, cattle-spearer and hunted outcast, sprang from uneasy sleep beside his stolen gin to snatch his spears as rumbling hooves bore down the dark creek bank from out the night.

In the shadows almost under the chestnut's belly he glared up, crouching motionless as the mob walked swiftly past and their hoof-beats grew dim in the great openness of the night.

The outlaw yabbered to his fear-stricken gin, his wild eyes dancing in a mad glee.

A swift black shadow in the night, he sprang off on a long twenty-mile run to a station homestead - Womera Jimmy, who wished to avoid white cattlemen more even than debil-debil.

A cleared space among the trees, a long, low shed of rough slabs in which were slung rows of untidy pack-saddles, close by the bark gunyahs of the sleeping aboriginal station hands. A larger building of slabs with the moonlight shining on corrugated iron, a light glinting from a rough window. The ordinary station homestead of a Cape York Peninsula cattle-run.

Inside, the "squatter" was seated at the slab eating table, beside him the withered form of the Chinese cook, opposite two white stockmen.

"We've had a great game tonight," yawned Brannigan as he put away the cards. "I don't remember when the station's been up so late before. What the - ?"

A furious baying of the station dogs, a crash, and the door flew open - the bound of something black as it sprang upon the table and kicked with naked, flying legs at the leaping, snarling dogs.

"Down, Bully! Down, Vixen!" roared Brannigan. "Kick Fang's ribs in, quick, Jack! They'll tear him to pieces!"

With kicks and curses the excited dogs were belted out of the room and the door slammed in the faces of the quickly gathering native stockmen.

Brannigan turned, breathing hard.

"By God!" he said. "It's Womera Jimmy! What were you up to, you black mongrel?" and he advanced threatingly towards the panting aboriginal.

"Me tellum - you - quick-fella, boss," Jimmy gasped.

"Big-Fella Burke - red fella - same fella catchem me two-fella year longa jail - him bad-fella white man - good-fella longa pleece - because he catchem me jail - him stealem plenty, *plenty* cattle - belonga *you*! Me see him - him travel longa Kendall - quick-fella - longa night-time."

Brannigan sat down slowly. "Take your time, Jimmy," he said, "get your wind. So long you tell em me true-fella, me givem you plenty flour, plenty tea, sugar, bacca, blanket, lettem you go altogether. You work longa me, sposem you like. Jack," he added quickly, "hustle the boys to run in the saddle horses. Lively now! You'd better go with them - they'll be scared of the dark.

An hour later the three whites and two black stockmen swung into saddles.

"Just in case we should get parted," said Brannigan, "I'll tell you the plan of operations. They daren't take the beasts along the overland telegraph line, they'd be seen. The only other way is through the Kendall Gorge and down the west coast, then over the Palmer Range, and down the Mount Carbine side. There's practically not a soul for two hundred miles. Our one chance is to block them just as they enter Kendall Gorge. It's their only outlet to the open country. The game is in our hands. We can travel by day. They daren't, for fear of stray niggers spotting them. The gorge is thirty miles away. We'll be waiting for them as they cross the Kendall tomorrow night."

With visions of a three thousand pounds' cheque and the lights of Sydney in the rear, Burke and his mates headed for the huge black gap that marked the narrow, seven-mile long gorge through the mountains. Beyond that stretched safety in no man's land.

The Kendall waters, like moon-kissed silver, flowed past the gorge mouth. The cattle, wild beasts, thirsty and frightened, smelt water and began to low, travelling fast. Burke cursed them for what they were, held the breakers back all he knew and encouraged the tiny band of trained "coachers" that walked so steadily in the van.

Often some startled beast would make a wild get-away from the flank, to be rounded back instantly by superb horsemanship on the part of both flanker and horse.

Rumbling down the boulder-strewn banks, the vanguard was pressed harder and faster by weight of bovine stupidity from the rear. In the stream's centre the loud splashings ceased as the beasts bent eagerly to drink. From out the blackness of the gorge mouth opposite five horsemen rode in open file, but abreast. They halted, and the moonlight glinted coldly blue on rifle-barrels even as Red Burke called back cheerily over the mob. "The worst is over now, boys. They've got no hope of ever seeing this beef again - except in tins."

A man on the flanks laughed.

"Just let 'em drink well. It'll steady them a bit." Several beasts, replete and satisfied, began horn-play. "Right," called Burke.

"Keep the mob well closed up. We don't want to lose any telltale strays at the mouth of the gorge."

The mob forged, splashing ahead, grunting their way up the sloping bank.

"Halt!" Burke instantly half wheeled his horse as the stem command snapped from the very sky.

"Throw up your hands! Lively, you're surrounded and covered!"

The cattle pressing on were jammed against Burke's horse. The loss of two months' hard work and risk flashed through his brain, criss-crossed with the lightning thought of just one chance. He swung into the saddle and shouted wildly, "Quick, quick, boys! Stampede the mob after me hell-for-leather down the gorge! We'll ride 'em down!"

Spurs bit deep into the chestnut's flanks. It bounded forwards. Instantly stockwhips cracked as the flankers galloped lashing and yelling among the cattle. Cat-calls, mad yells, sudden frightened bellowings shattered the silence of the night. The mob surged instantly forward on the trot, then in an unrestrained gallop.

"Fire at his horse!" yelled Brannigan. Three scarlet flashes stabbed the night - the gorge mouth crashed with echoes. The chestnut screamed, reared, and was borne down under a wild stampede of uncontrollable hooves.

Brannigan and his men put spurs to their mounts and, wheeling, galloped into the blackness with massed hooves at their horses' heels. The stone-paved gorge caught up thundering echoes and flung them against the rock-girt walls that quickly roared in an ever-increasing inferno of sound.

Trusting entirely to their terrified horses Brannigan's men galloped as even they had never galloped before.

Half-darkness bit the light from the towering narrow walls; dim grey shapes of boulders flashed by, only seen when passed; hissing sparks flew from iron-shod hooves, The gasping breath of the riders, the whistle of wind past the ears, half-glimpsed water pools and a man's eyes staring, his mouth wide, every tense muscle braced for the spring to roll beside a boulder when his horse surely must come down. One chance in a hundred then of escaping the thundering hooves behind.

Barely twenty minutes and the gorge walls lowered, widened out. The madly riding horsemen caught a Heaven-sent glimpse of open hilly country under the moonlight straight ahead.

"First chance you get swerve off and wait," yelled Brannigan. "Let the mob go on and shoot those --- pushing them on from behind!"

But though Brannigan's men waited until but distant grass-muffled thunder told of the still galloping mob, no riders came down the gorge.

"I know," said Brannigan finally, "they must have lost heart when Burke went down". He's pulp now. They've turned tail and made their get-away. We'll camp until dawn, then go after the mob. They'll be thirty miles away by then, blast everything!"

22

THE SLAYING OF RUNGOOMA

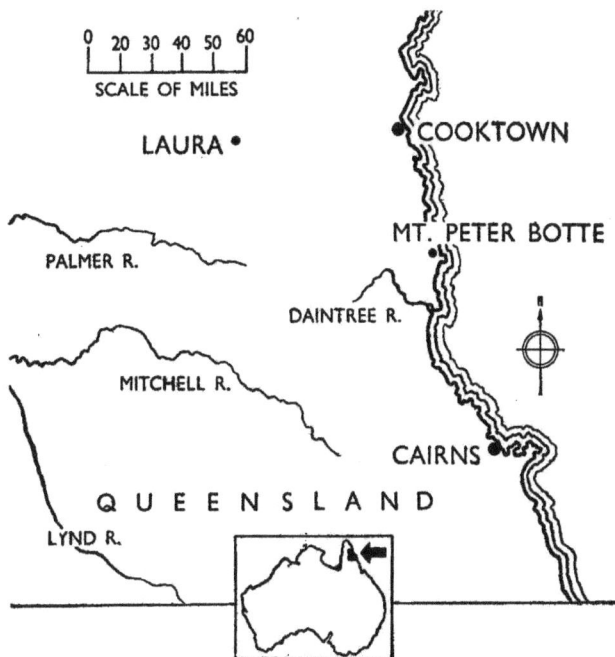

LITTLE humans that we are, almost eagerly we rush into judgments upon our fellow men, when often we cannot fairly judge our own selves. However, in this simple story, a factual story, I have judged Bunyarara, the young warrior, the hero-as he certainly appeared to me to be in my brave young days when this incident happened only a few miles from our jungle mountain camp. Yet reading over the old story, now that the vanishing years have brought grey whiskers-but, alas, so very little wisdom-it seems to me it was Wuroo, the miserable, harshly treated hunting dog that was the real hero. Or was it Hungooma the wild boar, roaming free in his own domains, sought out and forced to fight for the only thing that was his own in all this great big world-his life?

Judge for yourself.

The incident happened to one of the young warriors of the then numerically large Daintree River tribe of North Queensland, a bare forty miles north of Cairns. The actual fight took place up river, upon one of the densely timbered mountain ravines. In this isolation the only white men

151

were my two young mates and I prospecting for gold. The yelping of dogs brought us hurrying to the scene. The slaying of the notorious wild boar and the ripping open of the young warrior made a startling incident in our isolated lives.

Dark was the earth, and so still. At the foot of the range nestled a grassy sward now vivid within a circle of fires. Withered lubras and fat piccaninnies tended the fires - woe betide them should the flames not leap and dance.

Upon the sward danced a squad of stamping, hissing warriors. The flesh covering their skull and body bones was striped with white kaolin, lending a ghastly illusion of living skeletons whose frothing lips and gleaming eyes told of frenzy.

Within the squad danced the wizard-man, clothed in tufts of dyed grasses with brilliant feathers round his limb joints. From his scraggy neck swung his dilly-bag of charms, one hand flourishing the dreaded Death Bone, the other pointing at a grotesque figure on all fours which circled uneasily round him. The shambling figure was clad in a wild pig's skin which smelt warmly of fresh blood.

For on this day three wild pigs had fallen to the chase.

The warriors now were acting the events of the hunt before indulging in the feast already smelling pleasantly on the cooking stones.

To the screaming orders of the wizard-man the warriors leapt in the Hunt Dance, and on finding their prey rushed him with jabbing of spears and clashing of woomeras. At each growing climax the wizard-man would hastily place his hand on the pig-man, at which the warriors would reluctantly draw away and commence their circling tactics again.

Around the circle squatted the young lubras, their taut bodies massaged with goanna oil now a bronze sheen from the flames, teeth gleaming, black eyes flashing as they sang the chant and rhythm of the dance. A crooning chant, softly as the warriors glided in the hunt scene, increasing in volume as they found tracks of the quarry, rising to crescendo as they held their prey at bay, breaking into screams as they rushed in to give the death blows to a frenzy of drums.

The drum sounds were made by the young women, squatting upon their knees and sharply bringing their cupped hands down with a clapping motion between the thighs - a clear, sharp beat that echoed miles away in the ranges.

As the night wore on the motions of the dance worked the warriors into intense excitement. Eyes blazed from shaggy sockets, froth dribbled down the chins of youths and into the beards of warriors, spear arms twitched with the growing desire to kill. The wizard-man, expert in working up a frenzy, was becoming angry from the trouble he had to prevent them from actually spearing the cowering pig-man.

Suddenly Bunyarara, but recently initiated into warrior-hood, howled to the centre of the circle and rattled his fighting spears.

Instant silence - only the hum of the fires. Bunyarara screamed his challenge.

He would seek Rungooma, track him to his lair and spear him-alone! The warriors had the breasts of women! They were afraid! Was there one among them with courage game to go with him?

Only his panting breath broke the silence. Two circles of eyes focused upon him, those of the lubras alight with approval,

But Rungooma - the mighty boar that had already killed one warrior and crippled three others! Not a man moved.

Bunyarara lashed them with tongue and eye, and vowed he would slay Rungooma alone or never again dance at the fires. With a final howl of disdain he bounded through the circle and vanished.

A moment of listening, then warriors and lubras leapt and shouted loud into the night their frenzied approval. The wizard-man smiled quietly. Bunyarara sped through the night, long grasses swishing his legs. Soon he was among the foothills. The night air caressed him, cool as a mother's hand on the hot brow of her child.

He halted, glancing back. Through the darkness the fires blazed plainly. All around him was still, and big. The stars so high up there, so far, far away. He drew in a deep, awed breath. For suddenly he felt very, very small.

Bunyarara knew the spell of the dance was broken. The tribe would now be eating by the friendly fires, glancing uneasily into the darkness, whispering about his chance of return. With a scowl of bravado he shook his spears at the twinkling Barnes, turned, and walked on.

He peered suspiciously around him, superstitious fears already whispering. Why had he not waited until the Sun God awoke before hunting Rungooma? For then the spirits of the dead would be at rest.

His pace slackened. Before him was the steep spur that led right up to where the crown of the range kissed the very sky. Gazing up thus, he saw the tree branches in silhouette far above; a merry star was surely resting upon one towering branch.

He padded softly on. How the Wind Spirit kissed the grass tops with whispering breath! Suddenly the grass tufts slipped beneath him and he crashed down into a washed-out crevasse. For seconds his heart drummed within the narrow place. Then the black walls seemed moving in upon him. With an animal-like whimpering he sprang up the bank and snatched at the grasses above.

Lying close by were two fallen boulders from the mountain. Bunyarara squeezed between the cold rock sides and lay very, very still, lest the spirits of the night smell and touch him.

When at last the Sun God awoke he tossed a ray of light down between the rocks. And just then Bunyarara yelled and wedged himself hard between the rocks. On the sound of an explanatory whimper he sprang up in laughing joy for crouching down behind him, gazing from beseeching eyes, was Wuroo, his hunting dog, which had tracked him and now was licking the soles of his feet.

The Sun God was tossing in fiery awakening from his grey bed above the range. Bunyarara pushed his scratched shoulders from between the rocks and scrambled out. Bunyarara was a warrior again and felt young and brave. And Wuroo, his hunting dog, was here.

But the black man's eyes gleamed as with twitching woomera he snarled down at the now abjectly crouching mongrel.

Wuroo, his hunting dog, had frightened him - had nearly frightened him. What right had Wuroo to lick his feet when he knew the dread spirits of the dead were about? He would kill Wuroo.

Grunting, he swung his woomera - and paused, as he saw far away below, past the foothills, slowly ascending, thin spirals of smoke. The lubras were lighting the cooking fires.

And Bunyarara remembered Rungooma. His arm sank slowly to his side. Wistfully he gazed down through the floating mists at the smoke. Why had he so foolishly boasted the night before? But for that, he would be cosily asleep in his gunyah while the lubras prepared the morning meal. He dared not return now. The warriors would jeer, would sneer at him.

At the thought he rattled his spears angrily towards the camp. But it was the young girls who would make his life a misery. They would make up his boast into song and sing it softly with downcast eyes for many moons. And the warriors would laugh deep down in their throats. And he, Bunyarara, the fiery young buck, would go mad!

Abruptly Bunyarara turned and commenced the ascent of the steep forest spur. His hunting dog, relief plain in its pale eyes, trotted behind.

An hour's stiff climb brought him to the range-top.

Here began the dense wall of tropical scrub. Bunyarara whispered a reluctant goodbye to the Sun God and plunged into the gloom. He dared not look back towards the misty smoke now so far below. He made straight for the acknowledged hunting-grounds of Rungooma, a precipitous ravine avoided by the tribe since the death of the hunting warrior

Bunyarara had no intention of tackling Rungooma. His primitive brain was vainly trying to think out a glorious tale of how he had engaged the dreaded boar in fight. Without some plausible tale he dared not return to the ridicule of the camp. But it must sound very real. And he must make tracks, and signs of the struggle, evidence that would deceive even the experienced hunters. It was all going to be very, very difficult. His shaggy-browed visage grew gloomy as the jungle as, with shoulders now bowed, on leaden feet he trudged despondently on. Oh, why had he been such a fool? Why?

Coming to the moisture-laden foliage at the ravine edge the instinct of danger enlivened him with the hot thrill of the hunt. He felt a man again. Sheltered by a beautiful palm, he leant well over, his piercing eyes searching deep down between the gloomy foliage-matted walls. Nothing living was visible, only a dark-green carpet below. Should he jump now he would alight on the fronds of tree-ferns and palm, of wild banana and cable vine and creeper and a sea of green things struggling for life in that chasm be¬low. High above him swayed the interlocked branches of the towering scrub trees.

Bunyarara whispered to his dog to descend, then cautiously climbed down, eyes glaring through the almost green air, searching the shrubbery, particularly at the shad¬owed butts. When on the root-matted floor he crouched, listening breathlessly. Over miniature cliffs and across mossy rocks there glinted water like rippling silver, its lilt a music sweet and clear. Otherwise, there was only the deep silence of the living vegetation. Bunyarara stepped noiselessly on, his favourite weapon gripped to the woom¬era, spear arm poised, shaggy eyes alight, ivory teeth glint¬ing as he drew hissing breaths of excitement. Wuroo nosed on just ahead, the bristles along his mangy back rising ominously erect.

While working through a maze of lawyer-vines Wuroo growled fiercely and Rungooma, plodding heavily down his own ravine, halted abruptly, glanced at the backing, snarling dog, then up at the startled black man but fifteen feet behind.

A moment three hundredweight of wild boar stood solidly there in the velvet gloom, an indistinct bulk of untamable strength, the little cold, fish-like eyes staring at the man, the big curved tusks protruding from the bestial jaws, red clay daubed on the long snout where he had been rooting for yams.

Bunyarara's belly turned faint. He could not run, the elastic canes of the lawyer-vines were curled to his very thighs. He must throw, quickly - and vitally. And the looped canes interfered with his spear arm in that short distance.

Despairingly he jerked his arm sideways in an endeavour to miss the impenetrable shoulder hide, then with a hiss of the breath sent the vicious spear into the neck of the boar. And instantly bounded into the air to clear the entangling vines while Wuroo rushed snarling forward into the path of the boar.

The beast's eyelids jerked open and he grunted surprisedly at the sting of the spear. Then he lowered his snout and charged.

Wuroo leapt aside as Rungooma tore through the twisted vines as if they were grass. A bouncing cane caught between his snout and the spear. The cane tautened and the spear-haft snapped close to the neck. Wuroo leapt at the boar's hindquarters and sank his fangs into that one vitally painful part and hung grimly back among the clattering vines.

Just one second too late, for Bunyarara was falling, his spears rattling among the canes. He snatched one as fearfully he wriggled to protect his belly, and the point took the onrushing boar in the chest, Bunyarara grunted to the great weight as the spearhead sogged a foot deep into the body; the haft snapped, and the boar's tusks ripped into Bunyarara's side. He screamed, but Rungooma the boar was screaming, too, yes, in bestial grunts of rage and agony at the searing fangs, red-hot with pain, crunching into his tender hindquarters. Bunyarara screamed again, trying to gouge a flaming eye while his other hand pushed desperately back against the slavering snout-as well might a baby try push back the pain-maddened goring of a bull. The gouging tusks ripped into the man's back and with the quick upward thrust two ribs snapped and shot up pink and white through the black body. Bunyarara screamed again and rolled over on his back. Instantly the curved tusks were buried deep within his entrails.

The boar wheeled then on the worrying thing whose fangs were jerking and tugging within his hindquarters. But as the snout wheeled round so did that frenzied thing behind. The boar's heavy grunts broke into maddened roars as he surged round and round, until with a throaty gurgle blood gushed from his snout, his heaving bulk quietened into horrid, panting gasps, in a shivering weakness his hindquarters came to earth, his massive forequarters sank heavily down. Bunyarara's last spear had pierced his vitals. While even yet Wuroo, that miserable little scarred, skinny, half-starved hunting dog hung grimly on, all tangled up amongst weight of boar and scarlet lawyer-canes, his own mangy body now sticky from the blood of the boar all mixed with the blood of his master.

Came a soft pattering of hurrying pads, an urgent sniffling. Then the silence broke to the frenzied howls of the tribal hunting pack as with slavering mouths they charged the dying boar.

Bunyarara's agonized face smiled in an ecstasy of happiness, for now he would not die alone. As the warriors surrounded him his glazing eyes looked towards the boar and his arm waved in feeble endeavour to enact the scene - his last scene.

Now he would for ever be a great warrior. In lone fight he had slain the dreaded Rungooma and avenged the spirit of his tribesman. For ever now at the campfires the honour dance would be "Bunyarara slaying Rungooma". The warriors and young women would perpetuate his name in song for ever.

Thus Bunyarara slipped to the hunting-grounds of his fathers with a smile upon his lips.

23

THE BIG TOE OF WU-ROO-MOO

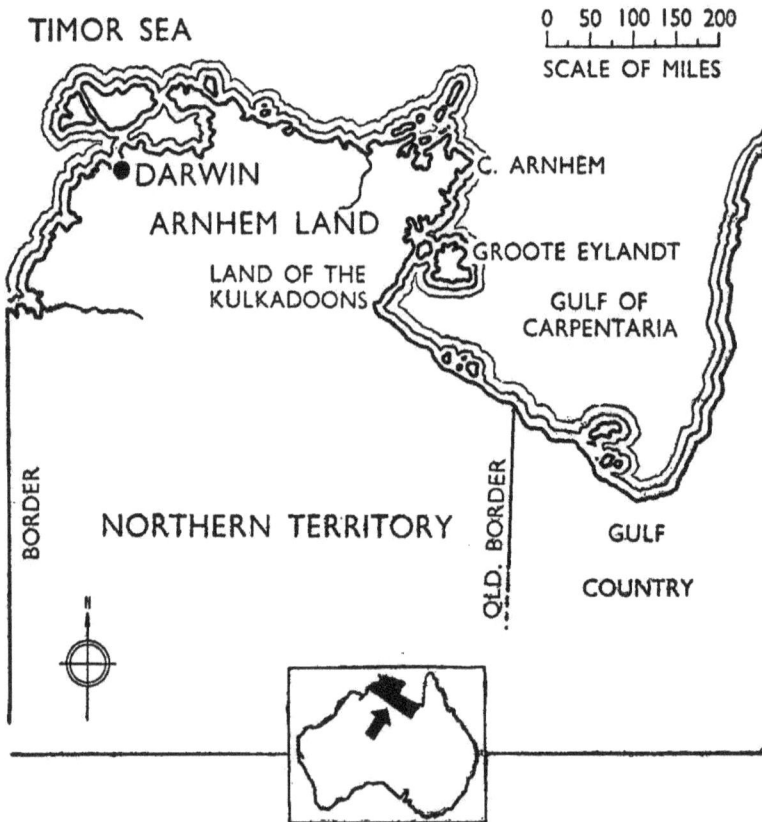

ALAS! This story is only too true.

Squatting on a cypress log was Wu-roo-moo, solemnly chopping off some toes, With casual, claw like fingers he stretched out the little toe of the left foot and held it solidly against the log, before striking down with the tomahawk. "Thump!" then the next toe, and "Thump!" again, until he came to the big toe.

Wu-roo-moo took more pains over that big toe than over the others. He seemed loath to part with it, for it was his climbing toe, a valuable toe. He only had one big toe left now It was not a messy job. There was but little blood, no panic cry of pain. Just chopping toes off, that's all, useless toes without feeling. Lately they had crinkled under-foot like lumps of shrivelling putty. They caught in the twisted grasses as he walked among the threadlike vines of the scrub; they were like wobbly fish-hooks, limply curling, impeding his progress. They were beginning to affect his living, too, for his stealth in tracking game was sometimes baffled at the critical moment by a toe dragging in a twig.

Wu-roo-moo picked up the putty-coloured lump of meat that was his big left toe. He examined it proudly but ruefully, as a man might gaze upon a glory that is past. Many a tall tree had that toe helped him climb, many a bees' nest and possum and squawking baby cockatoo had it helped to his cooking fire.

Well, he still had one big toe left. He gazed pridefully at the member with its hornlike toenail, a big squat toe, a black toe, tougher than leather beneath and far more pliable, a toe possessed of strength and a clinging leverage, with a cunning grip that was almost thought power.

Boastfully Wu-roo-moo stroked that living toe. To him it was as valuable as the strength of his spear arm and the quickness of his eye; he could never starve while he possessed those three good friends, and the breasts of Wy-mee would always be full for that greedy little piccaninny who called him father.

Wu-roo-moo stood upon his feet, feeling the leverage of the earth with his one big toe. Little did Wu-roo-moo understand that the strength of that dirt-encrusted toe was alive with the germs of living death.

As he walked away, surprise lightened his shaggy face at the awkwardness of his foot. His body felt strangely over-heavy; he could no longer tread with the panther-like grace that snaked him at times to within almost touching distance of the wild things of the bush. He trudged on doggedly, with his animal-like brain puzzling at the effect, never for a moment realizing that there was a cause.

He was a magnificent animal, this survival from the rude stone age, over six feet tall, with muscle-rippled chest and limbs sinewed in splendid strength. He was powerful enough to put up a fight even against a crocodile, if need be. His eyes, too, could follow the flight of an insect unerringly; his mind so tireless that he could travel straight "bush" for a hundred miles and only feel healthily tired on the morrow. That was before he lost his first big toe!

He represented Nature's first masterpiece. But he could not think-that is, he could not .reason, not as we understand the term. He could chew over the things of the past, over the things taught him by Nature and hard necessity, but he could not see "past his nose". He had reached the apex of his class; he represented man in a cul-de-sac. On earth at least he would never advance further towards the unknown goal our reasoning life is constantly forcing humans to strive for.

A tiny hole in a dead wattle-tree caught this wild man's eye. He limped towards it with delight in his shaggy eyes as he took his axe from his girdle. It was a flint-headed axe, ground sharp by concentrated labour and time and patience. The haft-end was split and in this the axe-head was securely thonged with kangaroo sinews.

That axe was a prized heirloom. Wu-roo-moo prized it even more highly now that it had cut off his big toe.Wu-roo-moo had killed two men with that axe; his father had killed three. His girdle was of the plaited hair of Wy-mee. She had made it for him. He loved the girdle, though not understanding why.

With strokes that rang through the forest he cut into the hollow of the wattle-tree, cunningly ripping the wood with the grain so that it whizzed away in slender splinters.

The bees buzzed into his eyes and his grim, deep-lined face, a face looking as if it had been roughly chiselled out of black stone. He did not notice them. So cunning was he with the axe that he hardly crushed one splinter into the honeycomb, nor did he waste one blow. He tore up a handful of broad-leafed blady grass, and with one twist round his wrist turned it into the shape of a bird's nest, carefully placing the honeycomb within. Hardly a cell of the golden honey was broken. He smiled as he thought of his honey sweetly melting among Wy-mee's lily-white teeth. He liked Wy-mee quite a lot, she was his woman - his first woman. He picked up his axe and departed, for the Fire God was retiring behind the range and throwing lengthening shadows that warned of the early coming of the spirits of the night.

Wu-roo-moo threw his game at the feet of Wy-mee - a bandicoot and a squirrel. Wy-mee was squatting by a little fire, her cooking leaves ready spread, her baby sucking its fingers upon her knees. Her dreamy eyes shone at the sight of her lord; he was kind to her.

He held one hand behind his back, glaring down with savage pride outlined upon his face. She gazed up silently, her eyes luminous. He brought forth the grass nest. The baby instantly thrust up greedy paws, chuckling in expectant delight. Wy-mee put the honeycomb in big lumps down to where it would do most good, licking her fingers as she quietened the greedy howls of her cub with a lump now and then. When the last taste was gone Wu-roo-moo pridefully dangled his big toe before his wife. She gazed at the trophy quite silently. She had seen the like before. But the piccaninny reached out greedily.

Wy-mee threw the game on the cooking coal, stirring up the hot ashes over and around it with the fire-hardened end of her yam-stick. An aroma of singed fur tingled the family nostrils. Wu-roo-moo grunted and squatted down to wait, screwing up his face as he feelingly scratched his back.

Night stole over the forest, bringing a chilly silence.

A bush rat ran across the dry pandanus leaves and they rustled distinctly. A beetle with big wings buzzed over the fire and away into the gloom. The piccaninny was gruffly warned, and its animal instinct immediately hushed its whimperings to a wide-eyed, listening silence. A mopoke croaked hoarsely from away up the valley, answered five minutes later in gruff croak from the hills. Star reflections gleamed down from the branches above. A peaceful hush camouflaged the bush.

But Wu-roo-moo, despite his immobility, was listening intently. No prowling enemy could see them, and the wood Wy-mee so economically burnt gave forth but a vanishing smoke that was not scented. But the smell of roasting flesh could betray them to possible enemies.

This tiny valley of the Little Lagoon was Wu-roo-moo's private hunting-ground. The tribe were camped miles away on the wild sea coast, raiding the mangrove swamps for crab and fish. Wu-roo-moo had chosen this valley because there he was sure of food for Wy-mee during the piccaninny's first babyhood. The tribe humoured him, the cicatrized scars of warriorhood wealed across his body advertised him as a man it was well to humour. It was the law, though, that he must rejoin the tribe in time for the totemic ceremonies due with the coming of the moon. So Wu-roo-moo brooded motionless in his lonely protection of his family, his hand itching for the quartz-tipped spears beside him.

Wy-mee poked the cooked food from the fire, flicking off the larger cinders with adept fingers. Wu-roo-moo seized the bandicoot and savagely tore it in pieces, eating in hungry gulps, and chewing the bones as a child would crunch toffee. Now and then he grunted, deep down. Wy-mee devoured the squirrel to the last little bone of its tail.

For some little time they sat staring at one another, at the fire, hearkening to the whisperings of the night. Through the trees, over a grassy point, was just one blue glimpse of the sea by day. By night, sometimes, when the wind spirit slept, the sea whispered to them. Wy-mee liked to stare at the sea. Far away across its mistiness lay Groote Island, the home of her forefathers. It called to her tonight in the whisper of the sea. Her liquid brown eyes were dreaming, her small face moulded still and rounded by memory's fingers. She lived over the dawn of the Kulkadoon raid, the sudden, terrifying war-howl, the awakening to the rush of skeleton-painted figures, the screams, the snarls of fighting men, the thud of blows, the grunting moan that echoed the breaking of bone and flesh. How she had sunk her teeth into the thigh of Wu-roo-moo and brought him squirming to the ground! She soon had loved her ravisher and made him love her by those intangible wiles which conquer the strength of men.

The thoughts of night vainly strove to breed constructive vision into the destructive mind of Wu-roo-moo. He did not think, but he was glowing with pride that he was a warrior of the Kulkadoons. Fiercest tribe in Australia and very numerous, even today they do not know the curb of the white man, those strange nomads with the thunder-sticks. Wu-roo-moo had no doubt whatever that the infrequent white strangers would come and go, as others had, leaving their grim land inviolate to the destiny of the Kulkadoons.

The Kulkadoons had given short shrift, when they could, to the old-time Chinese junks that came fishing for *beche-de-mer* in the troubled waters of the Gulf of Carpentaria. Wu-roo-moo did not understand that in material life death is ever-present though invisible. He never dreamt that death is everywhere - it never dies. He would never realize that it could seek him even through those long-dead yellow men. To him they were ended immediately his forefathers clubbed them. He could never have understood that they had left behind a living death. For before they had put him on the cooking fires a Chinese sailor who had tended the curing-shed a season away across on Groote Island had taken to wife the mother of Wy-mee. And Wy-mee had seen her mother's toes go like those of Wu-roo-moo, who did not know, nor did Wy-mee understand.

Wu-roo-moo thought boastfully of the proas of the Malay men who had harried his country's shores. These proas came no more, and Wu-roo-moo attributed it all to the invincibility of the Kulkadoons. He never dreamt of the customs dues of the white men, and their fast little ships that had ended the Malays' poaching.

Little brown men had been coming for long now. But they were wary of approaching the shores; Wu-roo-moo himself had savagely helped in the massacre of more than one lugger-load of these fighting little brown men who sought for the pearl-shells of the sea.

Eventually they must all vanish, leaving the Kulkadoons lords alone of the land, as their spirit ancestors were of the air.

Wu-roo-moo could never have understood that inevitably this great Arnhem Land had reached a period of its history when it must breed whites, when the last of the Kulkadoons must vanish to the spirit shades of his father. Ask Nature why. Even the great white man cannot answer. He cannot answer the riddle of where he is going himself. Perhaps Death smiles understandingly as he works on the second big toe of Wu-roo-moo.

24

THE BLOOD HOLE

TIMOR SEA

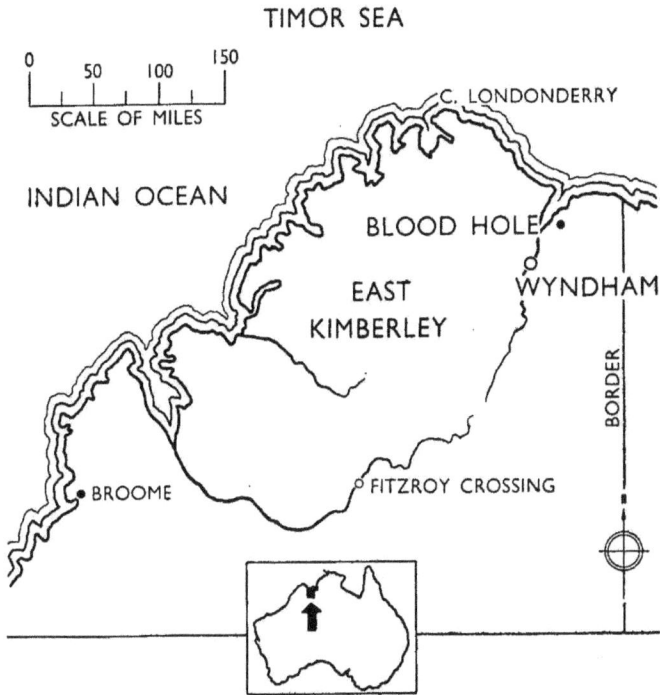

MERELY a page from my diary of the day. Since the afternoon that this was written many thousands of crocodiles along that coast have been shot for their skins.

Hideous brutes!

Evening.

All afternoon I have been sitting by the Blood Hole.

Mangroves to the brown water's edge; thick mud. Near a vaguely glimpsed opening in the mangroves little mullet swim close inshore, timid of enemies.

Cockatoos are screeching, fluttering like big white flowers on the green mangrove tops. Out on the broad waters is anchored the one resident vessel of Wyndham, the pilot launch. Away across the Gulf stand green and brown the trees and hills of the westward side, from which strike back the rays of the afternoon sun to gleam into the Blood Hole. Uncanny reflection. From away back behind the mangroves, and behind me, comes the dull hum of the Meatworks machinery.

Clinging to the muddy edge where the tide laps that leaf-shadowed opening in the mangroves Boats an arresting, dull, brickish-red scum.

It looks vaguely unhealthy, repulsive. It is blood-for the blood drain from the Meatworks gurgles trickling into here. And now the irresistibly rising tide holds the heavier fluid edged to the mud, from whence it tries to spread as a great wide stain overwhelming the brown.

The life-blood from hundreds of slaughtered cattle is daily emptied here, and even the waters of Cambridge Gulf cannot wash it entirely away.

All is quiet. The hum of the Meatworks comes subdued through the trees. A little crab is burrowing in the mud.

Something appears, quite Silently-the head of a crocodile.

But only the vague knobby top of it, like floating seed-pods upon the water; the tip of the snout is there now, the horny ridges of the eyes, cruel eyes, deep-set. It rises a fraction more and the serrations along the top of the tail appear. Even so, it is barely visible. No one would see it if he had not been expecting it. Its cold eyes are surveying things; it must hear, too, the noises of the earth, the screech of cockatoos, the faint clang of a hammer back at the Meatworks, the distant rattle of a bucket from the launch out in the Gulf. In deathly stillness it surveys the sombre shoreline. It knows a rifleman may be lurking there. It sinks.

Twenty minutes dream by; something appears quite suddenly away out on the water; where the placid calm is so slowly staining over is now again a knobby head, a long, serrated tail. The snout is turned inshore, the tail lazily moves, keeping the ugly body headed shorewards. Another rises beside it. They gaze towards the mangroves. Nothing moves, not a sign of life. With a lash of tail they chase one another round and round in slow enjoyment. A cockatoo screeches harshly; they vanish.

Now the tide begins to run out and the blood slowly follows it, the never dying stain growing gradually redder. A big fellow is coming now for his sundown meal. A horrid thing it is, as it slides in amongst the blood.

Through the flabby flaps in their gullets the big fellows force air with a grunting, gurgling sound as they jerk their snouts clear of the water. They laze in the blood drain with horrid mouths open while slimy fragments of gristle and refuse come drifting down to them. This refuse of the great slaughter they dreamily sift in their open snouts. When the hideous jaws are clogged full they lift their heads to the sky with a slow, jerking swallow.

Two hours drift by; the sun is sinking; half a dozen crocodiles have risen to stare towards the shore. With the falling of the water the blood is coming thicker. Mud-banks have crept into vision as the water recedes. Suddenly something brightly pink glows under the water twenty feet out from the shoreline. . It has grown to the size of a submerged blanket, it colours with the pinkness of a rosy sunset. Just as fast as the tide recedes, so does this pink blanket spread and grow. It is blood. Very slowly it turns russet, it must be coming from some drain outlet under the water; it spreads momentarily more strongly as the waters recede. Another crocodile comes up, gazing shoreward. He stays longer, he knows the sun is going down, darkness is coming. The russet turns to blood red, undiluted now as it creeps out from the muddy edge, gurgling after the receding water. It travels now with an uncanny swiftness, its long, crimson, pencil-like feelers creep along the mud edge and out into the mouth of that slimy inlet.

Sunset has come. A gorgeous sunset, a rosy flash of pink. It bathes the horrid snouts of many crocodiles. As the rose colour fades to dusk they are right in among that darkening pink dribbling out from the shore. One coughs harshly, there sounds the lash of a tail. Night has come.

Evening once more.

This morning was calm, high tide, the water high over the outlet of the blood drain, lapping in among the mangroves, the cloud in the water a rich pink. Very still was that cloud, for the tide that held it back was stationary. Under the just risen sun the mangrove shadows on the water were in cameo. A cockatoo screeched. On the outskirts of the cloud the water assumed a yellowish tinge and through this appeared long ribbons of darkish brown, many of them stretching right back among the mangroves.

A crocodile lay almost motionless in the centre of the " pink cloud, his snout-tip, his eyes, his serrated tail a brown-grey blob bathed in that rich pink.

Almost imperceptibly the cloud began to spread with the turn of the tide. As the tide moved, slowly the cloud crept in, drifting shorewards. Now were visible, gently floating through it, crimson clots of blood, like rich red plums. These were what the crocodiles lay open-mouthed for, to strain between their fangs. When one had his mouth nearly full his head, jaws partly open, would rise from the water. He would "blow" with a hoarse, throaty rattle, then swallow, then sink down again.

The edge of the pink cloud drifted down deep into the water; as it swayed in tenuous movement these edges spread like the fleecy drapery of clouds. A silver garfish swam with darting movement through the pink. A lane opened out behind him, a criss-crossy lane that came lazily rolling in again, rich, barely moving, slow walls of pink. The cloud edges, drifting ever more as the tide gradually gained way, now swayed to ever more beautiful cloud effects, drifting and gathering strength and floating away as a cloud might under a blood-red sun; only this cloud did not fade away, it was ever replenished.

Not even the bellow escapes at Wyndham. Death falls too swiftly. As the goaded cattle stumble up their Bridge of Sighs, each beast is met at the top by the man with the hammer. It drops with awful swiftness. In twelve minutes the beast is frozen beef - lightning speed.

No wonder the crocodiles are fat. Waste blood of thirty-three thousand bullocks gurgles down the blood drain each season.

But nothing is wasted.

Down at the Blood Hole the crocodiles wait. Fat fellows, greasy, slimy, slit-eyed, heavy jowled.

ETT IMPRINT has the following ION IDRIESS books in print in 2023:

Prospecting for Gold (1931)
Lasseter's Last Ride (1931)
Flynn of the Inland (1932)
The Desert Column (1932)
Men of the Jungle (1932)
Drums of Mer (1933)
Gold-Dust and Ashes (1933)
The Yellow Joss (1934)
Man Tracks (1935)
Over the Range (1937)
Forty Fathoms Deep (1937)
Madman's Island (1938)
Headhunters of the Coral Sea (1940)
Lightning Ridge (1940)
Nemarluk (1941)
Shoot to Kill (1942)
Sniping (1942)
Guerrilla Tactics (1942)
Trapping the Jap (1942)
Lurking Death (1942)
The Scout (1943)
Horrie the Wog Dog (1945)
The Opium Smugglers (1948)
The Wild White Man of Badu (1950)
Outlaws of the Leopolds (1952)
The Red Chief (1953)
The Silver City (1956)
Coral Sea Calling (1957)
Back O' Cairns (1958)
The Wild North (1960)
Tracks of Destiny (1961)
Gouger of the Bulletin (2013)
Ion Idriess: The Last Interview (2020)
Our Flying Aces (2023)

www.ingramcontent.com/pod-product-compliance
Lightning Source LLC
Chambersburg PA
CBHW030934090426
42737CB00007B/432